The RATIONAL INVESTOR

Common Sense Advice for Winning in the Stock Market

Edward F. Mrkvicka, Jr.

PROBUS PUBLISHING COMPANY
Chicago, Illinois

© 1991, Edward F. Mrkvicka, Jr.

This publication is designed to provide accurate and authoritative information in regard to the subject matter covered. It is sold with the understanding that the publisher and the author are not engaged in rendering legal, accounting or other professional service.

The publisher and author cannot be held responsible for any loss incurred as a result of the application of any of the information in this publication.

Library of Congress Cataloging in Publication Data Available

ISBN 1-55738-194-1

Printed in the United States of America

KP

1 2 3 4 5 6 7 8 9 0

This book is dedicated to my wife Maddy and our children Eddie and Kelly.

Acknowledgements

---

l would like to thank the entire staff of our newsletter *Money Insider* for the help and dedication that enabled this book to become a reality.

Contents

Preface

————

Each year dozens of new investment books appear. Hopeful consumers buy thousands of copies, and every year the results are the same. At best, the reader loses potential profit. At worst, they lose everything.

Why does this happen? First of all you have the volatility of today's financial markets. Rapid change makes yesterday's hot tip today's investment joke. Consequently, by the time an investment procedure is committed to book form it is outdated and useless.

Then you have the problem of generic investment advice. Simply stated, what's good for one investor isn't good for another. There are many aspects of the equation, such as: what are the investors' risk capital structures, what do they hope to accomplish with their investments, what are their short- and long-term expectations, and do they need capital growth or monthly income? Good investment advice starts with the premise that there is no single answer to the question of how to achieve investment success. That's why most general advice is dangerous.

Another problem with most investment advice is that it involves an attempt to predict the market. Investment decisions based on predictions don't work. The Crash of '87 proves that point.

Finally, and most important, you must consider the instability of any specific investment vehicle. Regardless of what you invest in, the principle of any known investment technique is not reliable. These plans don't allow for the inevitable, constant change.

Rational Investing is designed to avoid these problems and to put control of your investments back where it belongs: with you. It is as safe as any investment system can be. It requires no dollar minimum. It can be started within a few hours. It doesn't require excessive amounts of time. It doesn't expect you to predict the market or pretend to predict it for you. It doesn't rely on a particular type of market or investment vehicle. And it gives you the best return on your money.

Sound too good to be true? It isn't. Sometimes the simplest, most productive systems are the hardest to see. But, once you understand them, they keep proving themselves. That's been my experience with Rational Investing, and it will be yours too.

This program works because it starts where no one else has ever been. It doesn't try to figure out the market, and its basis is in the management program, not the investment vehicle choice. That approach ensures profit, regardless of changing circumstances. It works for any investment: mutual funds, stocks, commodities, gold, silver, real estate, bonds, or rare coins. It gives you the information you need to be your own expert and avoid the costly mistakes others are making. It doesn't require outside influence to make it work, which means you don't have to waste time worrying about what keeps many investors up at night. In a good market it works. In a bad market it works. Actually, the volatility of the market works to the plan's advantage. These are just a few of the qualities that make Rational Investing unique.

Historical statistics make clear that the odds of investing successfully are scant at best. *The Rational Investor* changes those odds, because it ignores all the trappings that cause the others to fail. It simplifies the complicated, and it turns losing investments into winners. It is the one plan that beats the system.

Your investment potential is about to become unlimited.

Edward F. Mrkvicka, Jr.

PART I

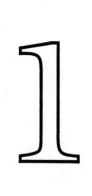

Are You Right for the Market?

Investing, in a general sense, is the employment of capital in the expectation of monetary gain. The vehicle in which you invest is unimportant. Mutual funds, stocks, bonds, savings accounts, real estate, businesses, and precious metals can all qualify as investments.

Many tend to confuse investments with speculation. That confusion causes them to be disappointed in their results. To clear the air, an investment is made in anticipation of long-term capital gains and possible short-term income. A speculation is made in anticipation of short-term capital gains. So the next time you hear someone talking about investing in the commodity market, you'll know you are dealing with a person who has no idea of what he is doing, at least from an investment perspective. You don't invest in commodities, you speculate. This may seem to be a matter of extraneous semantics, but it's important to understand what the difference represents. It means that many people investing in the market today can't possibly meet their financial expectations since their very understanding of the process is flawed.

Investments, in a general sense, should have virtually no possibility of substantial capital loss, whereas speculation has not just the possibility, but the probability. Nevertheless, risk-exposure speculation entices many because of the chance, albeit remote, of immediate and sometimes sizable gain. Before the market bug bites you, remember that most trades made by individual investors are losers. In fact, the win/loss ratio of the individual investor is so skewed it defies common sense and mathematical logic. Those who enter the marketplace are not playing on a level field. The pros control the market, and the amateurs are at a planned disadvantage.

The necessity of Rational Investing becomes more apparent as one reviews the market as it really exists. You have to play with different rules than individual investors usually use or you are going to lose, lose big, and lose consistently. That's the way the market is structured.

So, let's assume you know how different financial vehicles work and you've determined what your personal investment objectives are. You are still faced with a serious obstacle. Yourself. Even if you've established your market or investment vehicle choice, should you, with your personality, be investing there? Are you doomed to failure from the start? I am not talking about the market now; I am talking about you. Take a boxer with a glass jaw. He may love the sport, but regardless of his dedication and training he will always be a loser. The sport isn't right for him. That can happen to investors too.

That's another reason Rational Investing is so valuable. It takes into account what most programs don't— that the individual personality of the investor is a critical factor in the success or failure of any investment strategy. Not all investors belong in the same market. For example, some speculators should not be in foreign currencies. Their constitution will not be able to stand the strain. The volatility will cause them to make decisions based on personal characteristics instead of market signals. Some people, if they require a predetermined monthly income, should never leave the solid gold blue chips if they want to sleep at night. Everyone has a unique investment personality.

Sometimes these positions change. For instance, when a couple is starting out in life, they may wish to invest small sums in varying markets. As their net worth grows, they may opt to speculate with their risk capital while continuing to invest the remainder of their liquid capital. As they near retirement, they may decide to invest in long-term vehicles that will protect their income. Later, if one spouse passes away, the survivor may wish to continue a portion of the investment portfolio while making other arrangements for additional family members (e.g. trusts, wills, gifts). The point is that no one right way to invest exists. There isn't even one right way to invest for a specific person or couple. All things do not remain equal or stagnant. Needs change. The markets change. This variability is another reason why the plan is so very valuable. You can apply its principles in every situation.

You should never underestimate the role your personality plays in the investment process. You may have some traits or financial flaws that will make certain types of investing very difficult for you to profit by. You have to recognize these traits going out the gate or your plan, no matter how well conceived, will fail. Winning in the market is a combination of the market circumstances, the vehicle chosen, and the financial complexity of the individual making the decisions. I can't make your investment choices for you, and neither can someone else. But I can give you some insight into what characteristics make up the winners and losers in the investment field. See if you don't recognize some personality/investment traits of your own in Table 1.

TABLE 1
Personality/Investment Traits

Factor	Negative	Positive
Resources	Undercapitalized	Substantial capitalization. Can absorb losses. Lets winners ride.
Resource management	Seldom has reserve position	Always has long-term, sizable reserves
Self control	Emotional. Takes small profits, big losses	Reacts to market signals only
Market skill	Little market knowledge	Is either an expert or employs one (a broker doesn't necessarily qualify as an expert)
Market position	Single positions	Always diversified. Usually, no more than 10 to 20 percent in one market
Market education	Little knowledge. At best, relies exclusively on broker	Well-researched positions
Game plan	No plan. Constantly changing strategy	Cuts losses. Doesn't deviate from plan. Changes strategy only when events dictate
Timing	Only acts when broker calls, or gets hot tip from friend	Acts on market. Usually calls broker before broker calls him
Objectives	Wants to make quick killing	Long-term plan
Damage control	High risks. Positions are wiped out frequently	Uses alerts, stops, etc.
Market focus	Part-time attention	Full-time market follower. Devotes quality time to portfolio.

As you can see, it's not only the market, or what vehicle you choose, but also your investment personality that will decide whether you win or lose. If your temperament is ill suited to your investment choice, you will ultimately lose regardless of the success of the vehicle. Certain disciplines are required in certain markets. If you don't qualify you shouldn't be in that market.

I believe strongly that you can learn and make adjustments to fit your investment needs. However, I also believe that average investors, those that do not follow the markets full-time or as a career, will never be as prosperous with their investments as they should be. If you'll be honest, the table you just reviewed should have showed you one thing: you can't consistently win because you have too many negative traits. All part-time investors do. Of course, I didn't present the chart to show your strengths, but rather the inherent weaknesses of all part-time investors. It was my way of showing that the average person will, due to the nature of the system, lose money; it's just a matter of how much. The pros have all the positive traits. The rest of us lose because we have negative traits. In the market, "The big fish feed on the little fish." That's fact. If you can't admit that, you have a problem.

Where does that leave us? Clearly, you need an investment program that by itself repairs all your negative investment traits. Rational Investing is that plan. It helps solve every negative trait on the chart, and you don't have to do a thing. It also amplifies positive traits, which means it will enhance the pro's results too. More important, it will lead you in the general direction of your market. Rational Investing doesn't make a specific investment vehicle choice for you. That's your responsibility. You choose the investment vehicle and then apply the plan's formulas. Much of the book's information is geared towards helping you make that important choice. Don't confuse that personal decision with the plan. They are separate, yet as you will see, work hand in hand.

A GOOD INVESTMENT PROGRAM IS ONE THAT STANDS ON ITS OWN WITHOUT THE BURDEN OF THE PERSONALITY OF THE INVESTOR. Here are some guidelines to assist your investment decisions:

1. Have an investment plan only. You cannot afford to speculate.

2. Use risk capital only (money not needed for housing, food, etc.).

3. Diversification is required. The all-your-financial-eggs-in-one-basket approach is not prudent.

4. Review your positions. No investment can be allowed to become dormant.

5. Devote quality time to your investments. Time should not be measured by time per se, as the simplicity of Rational Investing will prove.

6. Become a professional. Your personal finances are important and deserve your full attention.

7. Never allow yourself to lose hands-on control of your investments (probably the most important rule of investing!).

A Rational Investor follows these recommendations, and so should you. You see, there is no such thing as the perfect investor. There is however a perfect investment plan, which is what this book offers. The smartest thing you can do with your money is admit your inability to beat a system designed by the few (the pros) to take from the many (the individual investors). That's why you need to rely on a program that has all the investing attributes most of us don't have. It's called Rational Investing.

2

Flexibility and Diversification

One of the principles of the plan, which I outlined in the introduction, is the importance of diversification. That's a word you've probably heard a lot, mostly from financial sales representatives trying to get you to diversify into their product. Quite possibly, you may think diversification is something only investors with large portfolios have to worry about. I'd like to spend a few pages impressing on you the importance of diversification for every investor, no matter how small their investments.

In our quasi-free market you have a constant guarantee that nothing is constant. That means the rate of inflation will go up, and the rate of inflation will go down. Interest rates will go up; rates will go down. Therefore, on the face of it, one specific approach to financial planning will not work. Circumstances will change, making a rigid plan successful only a portion of the time. That was true until now.

Even though Rational Investing, coupled with intelligent investment vehicle choice, will solve the problem of flexibility and diversification, it needs to be reviewed here. Why? To give you additional faith in the program. There are certain keys that it uses, and this is one of them.

No one can prognosticate exactly when changes in any market will occur, which means your reaction time is impaired. It also means you will lose some money along the way. Even if you react before the majority, you will react late in terms of the optimal moment. Long-term errors in this regard are even more costly. Let's use an example to show what can happen when a plan does not take into account changes that most assuredly will happen.

Consider the 1989 plight of the savings and loan industry. Fifteen years before, S&L's invested almost completely in low interest rate residential mortgages. When inflation increased to the teens and homes weren't selling because most could not afford the mortgage rates, the S&L's started going broke. And because they had a lock-in position, there was nothing they could do except watch. Then when the industry was deregulated, they went to the opposite end of the spectrum. The results are well documented. They weren't the victims of an economic cycle, they were the victims of management-designed and government-mandated inflexibility and subsequent over-reaction. They had originally invested as if nothing were ever going to change. They were wrong.

As the case of the S&L's illustrates, inflation can be a significant factor affecting your investments. But its long-term effects are often subtle and easy to miss. However, inflation can be beat if you have a flexible financial plan that is diversified, and that doesn't just mean investing in a number of different stocks.

Table 2 should make it more than clear that everyone must have some form of investment plan, a plan that

TABLE 2
What Today's $100,000 Will Be Worth

Rate of Inflation (%)	Today's Value ($)	Value in 5 Years ($)	Value in 15 Years ($)	Value in 25 Years ($)
6	100,000	74,726	41,727	23,300
8	100,000	68,058	31.524	14,602
10	100,000	62,092	23,939	9,230
12	100,000	56,743	18,270	5,882
14	100,000	51,937	14,010	3,779

takes into account all of the unspoken, inconspicuous aspects that might determine your success or failure. Having a plan that ignores inflation would be catastrophic. Regardless of individual success, the plan, in total, would fail. It should also be said that those who plan and are financially educated realize that in every general financial disaster there is individual opportunity. Never forget, many fortunes were made in the Depression too.

There is another pressing reason a portfolio must remain flexible. Quite often, as it was throughout most of the eighties, inflation is brought under control by government manipulation rather than authentic market forces, and people start believing that the inflation problem has disappeared. To some small extent they are right. But often in its place come new threats— or instance, the decline of the dollar. This occurance, the decreased purchasing power of the dollar, can be recognized by reviewing the cost of goods and services during any time span.

For example, according to the Government Accounting Office, the dollar of 1964 lost 70 percent of its purchasing power by the year 1988. I expect, based on continued government interference in our "free market," that the 1988 dollar will lose 80 percent, or more, of its purchasing power by the year 2000. That means the dollar's value will be twenty cents, or less, of its present depressed worth. We could be looking at an average car price of $75,000, or an average home price of over $535,000 in just twelve years. Although not a forecast, that's a very real possibility.

How did the price of goods and services go up so much during a time when inflation was under control? The alarming fact is, when the dollar is in decline the inflation rate is only measuring a small part of the problem. The overall decline in your purchasing power is perhaps three to four times larger than the inflation rate.

Although it's reassuring to read about a low inflation rate, it doesn't change the fact that during the same time prices may be escalating dramatically. You should be concerned with this dilemma because your financial future is being eroded in such a manner that you may not be able to discern the course of events. Each and every year you have less and less purchasing power. Only when you realize that sad financial truth can you plan a strategy that will produce financial success. Your investments have to ensure that your returns surpass the true cost of inflation and rising prices. Don't forget the inflation rate, but understand what it actually represents. On the other side of the coin, in many cases, the government further erodes the value of our currency by uncontrollably printing more worthless fiat money.

Given the unpredictable effect of government policies (e.g., inflation, a declining dollar) and their subsequent effect on your financial future, what can you do? Rational Investing takes into account economic unpredictabilities by giving up any attempt to predict. That may sound enigmatic, but it's not. If you worry about the uncontrollable you'll make additional mistakes. You will make decisions based on emotions, intuitions, feelings. The plan removes your subjectivity, your desire to be right about the market. This is essential for consistent profits. Your flexibility and diversification come into play with your investment vehicle choice, *not the plan*. This is critical. Your vehicle choice is open to debate based on your needs and expectations. The plan is rigid by design. That's to your benefit.

As to your vehicle choices, the inflation rate can be a guide. Ask yourself two questions: (1) Is the rate of inflation going up or down? and (2) Are interest rates going up or down? The answers to those questions can bring you the right selection of vehicles to choose from. When the rate of inflation is rising severely, coupled with a rise in interest rates, buy semiliquid hedge investments (gold, silver, mining stocks, selected mutual funds, etc.), or use your money market vehicle. Traditional savings should also be considered when interest rates are exceedingly high. When inflation is decreasing along with falling interest rates, buy market vehicles (stocks, mutual funds, etc.). Again, the choice of a specific vehicle is yours. This may appear complicated, but it's not. I'm telling you this so you see the necessity of protecting your finances from unseen forces like inflation and a declining dollar, and so you understand why various principles have to be part of your thought process when you decide which investment vehicle is right at any given time. At that point Rational Investing takes over. The plan and your careful investment choice are virtually unbeatable.

Winning Small, Losing Big

As every stock market investor knows, to win in the market you must limit your losses and let your winners ride. That's easier said than done. If it were easy to do, investors, all investors, would be constant bottom-line winners. That, as we know, is unfortunately not the case. Individual investors lose most of the time.

Knowing the odds are against you, you should realize that your losing trades, regardless of their number or frequency, must be monetarily limited. On the other hand, your winners, even though you probably have only a few, should be allowed to accrue the maximum profit potential. If you're a good trader you may have ten times the losers, but they should have a dollar total substantially less than what the few winners produce. That ratio is what results in market profit.

Why then, if no one contests that ratio, do individual investors continually lose money? I am not talking about speculators, but investors. The problem is human nature.

No one wants to admit to making a mistake. And then too, "You never know when things could turn around." Some people who allow their losses to run have an ego problem. They cannot deal with the realities of the market. Even those that do have a market strategy sometimes allow their emotions to rule their common sense. They then get into a contest of wills with the market. The market almost always wins.

For every investor that tries to buck the market, there's one who's scared of it. This can be just as costly. Knowing that an investment showing profit should run its course and allowing it to do so are two different things, especially if you've ridden a few too many losers recently. Many investors have a tendency to take what they can get, and offset their losses with immediate profit. Ego can also cause investors to sell too early. Many traders like to talk about their winners. They made money here; they made money there. They never bother to add it up, which if they did, would more often than not show a substantial loss.

Losing big and winning small is often caused by the investor's lack of financial education. Some people simply don't understand the entire market picture as it pertains to their portfolio. They either listen to their broker exclusively, or they become overly concerned with individual trades instead of overall results. In contrast, the smart investor realizes the only thing that matters is your net profit at year-end.

The rule is: limit your losses, and let your winners ride. That is all-encompassing, and by itself gives a dictate that cannot, and should not, be fine tuned. I admit that there are times that following this market axiom will cost you money. In fact, I can guarantee my readers that at some time your stop-loss order will be hit, and then the stock will turn around. But the safety a stop-loss order gives is worth the occasional loss. The most important thing is establishing the maximum you are willing to lose on a specific trade. That's what determines your stop-loss order. Being conservative here will not hurt. However, being overly conservative will, since you must be able to withstand small market swings. A stop-loss built too close to your investment entry price could result in too quick a sale.

What about the profit side? Here too, many go wrong because they never establish the stock's potential for gain. *There has to be a better than average potential for gain before the profitable investor will risk capital.* Investing in the market just to be investing in the market is a mistake.

The real key is to abide by the results of your determinations. Don't let pride or the results of past trades dictate your position. Just because you get out, or sell, doesn't mean you should necessarily abandon the investment choice entirely. Maybe you were right all along, but that doesn't mean you should ride out a purchase to make the point. Get out when required and then back in when circumstances indicate another buy. The pros realize that much can be gained this way, and they are not the least bit shy about retreating and then re-entering whenever called for.

What is a better-than-average profit potential? Your expectations will determine what you consider average, but generally speaking a return of 5 to 10 percent is not adequate to offset the long-term overall portfolio potential for loss. In fact, you should believe, based on research and knowledge, that your investment holds a foreseeable return of 50 percent or better. Shocked? You are if you listen to most brokers or market experts. But figure it out. You need that capacity unless you're infallible.

Refusing to enter any position without that potential will stop you from being rushed into stocks or any other vehicle by anyone, your broker included. Using my criterion eliminates most offerings, making your ultimate choice easier. Also, if you enter a position secure in the knowledge that your market potential is not overstated, you will not be tempted to get out with limited results. If you're expecting 50 percent (including growth and dividends), chances are you won't settle for something as small as 7 or 8 percent. That would help many of us.

If all there was to winning (in terms of year-end profit) were limiting your losses and letting your winners run, all investors would be winners. A market law of averages would indicate that any combination of investments would accomplish results. But, of course, no such law exists. If you pick twenty stocks, ten will not be losers and ten will not be winners. Most will be losers. That ratio presents an interesting problem. Not only do you have to pick the right stocks, you then have to manage the portfolio to maximize its potential. Many investors who consider themselves financially savvy confine themselves to, or only understand, picking the stocks. The fact is, *managing the portfolio is just as important, if not more so!* Rational Investing realizes that. Why? Because of the cumulative effect of market decisions. If you had a portfolio that did in fact have a 50 percent success ratio in terms of picking winning stocks, but your winners returned only an average of 5 percent while your losers returned a loss of 20 percent, you can see the end result. However, if your market homework and instinct were right only 15 percent of the time, and your winners returned 50 percent while the losers averaged 5 percent, you can see that end result too. The key, after investment vehicle choice, is portfolio management.

Your market reality has to coincide with a workable market strategy. If you know you should limit your losses and let your winners ride, why are you doing just the opposite? You cannot afford "Winning Small, Losing Big".

Fortunately, there are ways to bring your portfolio back into a profitable mode. Specifically:

1. Start looking at your investments on a portfolio basis. Individual trades are not unimportant, but they may mean little when all the dust settles.

2. Refuse to invest in any vehicle that does not have a return potential of at least 50 percent.

3. Appraise market potential in its entirety (growth, dividends, appreciation, etc.).

4. Remember, you're on an unlevel playing field, and as such, you have to make adjustments to balance your position. You're going to win only a few, so you'd better make them count.

5. A loss is a loss. By itself it means nothing other than you probably should be doing some more research. If your ego cannot stand the strain of admitting defeat, get out of the market before you lose it all.

6. The potential for future profit may be there even though your original investment positioning may have been flawed. Realizing that may help those with market egos. It may also help maximize profits for you market potatoes (those that invest and then sit forever with the same position).

7. The only thing that counts is year-end monetary results. Adding up the number of your winners and losers doesn't mean anything.

If you follow Rational Investing faithfully, it will solve these problems for you, since it takes your market ego out of the picture. It even lets you make money when things don't look so good. It functions as its own stop-loss order and its own profit protector, both of which are explained later. I have to warn you, however, that it accomplishes these important aspects of investing in a most contrary manner, as will become apparent in the chapter entitled "The Plan and How It Works". The fact remains: the plan reduces your losses, and increases your gains. On your own you might end up doing just the opposite.

PART II

4

The Importance of Investment Choice

Up to now I have been talking about general principles on which Rational Investing is based. I've claimed that these principles hold true no matter what market vehicle you choose. But you're probably still wondering where you should turn and what investments you should make. In this section, I'll offer some guidelines and specific information to help you make the most effective choices.

Your first obligation in the area of investing is to state your goals! The best investment, in terms of potential return, may be the worst for some individuals. Remember, if you're looking for a retirement portfolio in twenty years, you don't speculate in commodities. If you are looking for immediate capital growth, you don't invest in mutual funds. I have spent a lifetime consulting in the area of finance and investments, and the most common mistake the investor makes is not matching his or her needs and expectations to a vehicle that can achieve them.

Unfortunately, most investors never understand the relationship between personal goals and expectations and the instrument they choose. Regardless of the actual return, this misunderstanding guarantees nothing but disappointment. Even Rational Investing has personal limitations, and although it will always give a maximum financial return, it cannot make you happy if you didn't know what you were trying to accomplish in the first place.

Take a moment to list the attributes of the perfect investment, as you see it. Obviously, we should expect as many different definitions as people participating. But there should also be some highlights that we would find in most, if not all, of the outlines. For instance, most probably mentioned liquidity, inflation hedge, high rate return, monthly income, stability, and leverage use.

Regardless of the attributes of your perfect investment, it should have two important features: stability and strength. That may seem obvious, but let's look more closely at what those terms really mean.

Stability in reference to investments means that we have a reasonable expectation of continued growth, with little chance of wildly fluctuating returns or loss of capital. For most investors this is crucial. Stability is the line that separates the investor from the speculator. It allows planning for the future, which is important to long-term results.

Strength, as I use it here, may appear complicated. When it refers to investments, strength is the ability to leverage your investment. That doesn't mean you have to leverage all your investments (in fact you shouldn't), but nearly all your investments should have that capability. When additional money-making opportunities arise, you will be able to take advantage of them.

What investments meet the criteria of stability and strength? Let's review the typical investments considered by most. The following are the criteria I will apply to each investment choice:

1. LIQUIDITY: The ability to turn an asset into immediate cash without penalty.

2. STABILITY: Good profit potential with little associated risk.

3. STRENGTH (Leverage): The ability to re-use your asset.

4. INFLATION HEDGE: The potential to stay ahead of a rising inflation rate.

5. CASH FLOW: Income in the form of cash as opposed to equities.

6. MOBILITY: The ability to physically move the asset.

7. LIMITED MANAGEMENT REQUIREMENTS: Little time expenditure needed.

MONETARY INVESTMENTS:

1. SAVINGS VEHICLES (passbooks, CD's) = Liquidity, Stability, Mobility, Cash Flow, Limited Management Requirements.

2. GOVERNMENT BONDS = Liquidity, Stability, Mobility, Cash Flow, Limited Management Requirements.

3. MONEY MARKETS = Liquidity, Stability, Mobility, Cash Flow, Limited Management Requirements.

MARKET INVESTMENTS & SPECULATION:

1. STOCKS = Liquidity, Strength, Mobility, Cash Flow, Medium to High Management Requirements.

2. COMMODITIES = Liquidity, Strength, Inflation Hedge, High Management Requirements.

3. BONDS = Liquidity, Strength, Mobility, Cash Flow, Medium to High Management Requirements.

4. MUTUAL FUNDS = Liquidity, Stability, Strength, Mobility, Cash Flow, Low Management Requirements.

5. PERSONAL LENDING = Liquidity, Stability, Strength, Mobility, Cash Flow, Variable Management Requirements.

HARD COMMODITIES:

1. GOLD = Liquidity, Strength, Inflation Hedge, Mobility, Medium to High Management Requirements.

2. SILVER = Liquidity, Strength, Inflation Hedge, Mobility, Medium to High Management Requirements.

3. INVESTMENT COMMODITIES (stamps, antiques, etc.) = Stability, Inflation Hedge, Mobility, Low to Medium Management Requirements.

4. INVESTMENT COINS = Liquidity, Stability, Strength, Inflation Hedge, Mobility, Low to Medium Management Requirements.

CAPITAL INVESTMENTS:

1. PERSONALLY OWNED BUSINESS = Strength, Cash Flow, Very High Management Requirements.

2. PERSONAL LENDING TO OTHERS = Stability, Strength, Inflation Hedge, Cash Flow, Very High Management Requirements.

This categorizing should have opened your eyes to the potential of some investments and the limitations of others. The stock market, for instance, qualifies in the area of strength, but it lacks stability. Over time that means your chances of success are reduced by the very nature of the system. Its volatility means you may lose the vast majority of times. On the other hand, an investment like bank savings has the stability we need, but lacks potential for sizable profit in the short run.

There are other considerations for some investors. Liquidity may have added importance for you, and if it does, lending (personal and business) will not meet your needs even though they meet our stability and strength test. If getting to your money immediately is important, you have to trade qualities. This would be true of any other particular considerations you may have.

You may have noticed that there are really very few investments that qualify for your consideration, once all criteria have been taken into account. That shouldn't surprise you. Most investments are designed by the seller for their maximum profit, not yours. You need to be aware of this in making any investment decision.

This advantage to the seller means that any investment situation where you can be the seller, such as personal and business lending, may be a great opportunity. If you become your own expert/manager and put deals together, you will reap the best of stability and strength to produce wealth. Of course, most of us don't have the time that such ventures require.

I would be remiss if we didn't further examine investment vehicle safety. Sadly, too many investors, except in the most obvious cases, such as junk bonds, ignore the element of risk in their investment choices. However, they become acutely aware of this oversight when their choice starts losing money, but by then of course it's too late. You have to understand the inherent risk factor of a given investment vehicle prior to determining if it should be part of your portfolio. Your individual circumstances may cause you to accept higher than normal risk. That's fine, if in fact you understand that risk prior to committing a dollar of your hard-earned resources.

The following list reviews the more traditional investments, starting with the most secure and finishing with the most risky:

1. TREASURY ISSUES: Their undeniable safety factor cannot be argued against, for it would take a governmental collapse to make your investment worthless. In a worst-case scenario you would have other, more pressing considerations than concern regarding your investments.

2. FEDERALLY INSURED TIME CERTIFICATES OF DEPOSITS: As long as you don't exceed the insurance limits, these investments have the same bottom-line backing as Treasury issues; i.e., the full faith and credit of the federal government. Certificates of deposit are available through many institutions like banks, savings and loan associations, and credit unions. Note: I placed this listing according to its recorded safety performance. I refer you to the chapter entitled "What About Your Cash" for my opinion of government insurance.

3. GOVERNMENT SECURITIES: Considered safe for all the obvious reasons.

4. MUNICIPAL BONDS: As long as you have reviewed and are satisfied with the bond's rating, you stand little chance of losing your money.

5. MUTUAL FUNDS: Depending on your investment choices, you can be either safe or somewhat at risk. The safety factor is determined by your fund choice. Some are extremely conservative, whereas others are aggressive beyond what you may find acceptable. You have to do your investigative homework. Of course, since mutual funds must be diversified by law, you have added safety.

6. REAL ESTATE: In general, real estate is a safe investment. However, if you wander outside the norm into leveraged positions or into highly speculative property, you have defeated the safety factor. Real estate derives a large part of its safety through the investor's knowledge of the local market. The bottom line is this: real estate can be ex-

tremely safe and profitable or potentially dangerous. Your approach determines the odds.

7. PRECIOUS METALS AND NUMISMATIC COINS: Both have experienced up and down swings large enough to question their safety. That concern is well placed. However, precious metals and investment grade coins deserve this fairly high rating because they always have value. Unlike stocks and bonds, precious metals never become valueless. Consequently, if you can hold the investment you will probably recover most, if not all, of your loss. That can be said for very few investments.

8. CORPORATE BONDS: You must use a rating service before buying a corporate bond. But, once you do, you have set a fairly high standard of safety, assuming you opt for only those of exceptionally high ranking.

9. STOCKS: The stock market can be either a safe haven for your investments or awash with risk. Like mutual funds, it's not the market per se that determines safety, rather the individual choices of the investor. For instance, you're on fairly solid ground with IBM, but you may be on shaky ground with a new, unproven issue.

10. MARGIN TRADING: Although margin trading is still in the stock market, you are exposing more money than you have invested since you have borrowed money to make the purchase. Then, of course, there are the infamous margin calls. Here too, depending on your stock choice, you have a predetermined element of risk coupled with the added exposure of the margin itself.

11. OPTIONS: Stock options allow you to buy at a known price, on a given date. The risk factor is obvious. If the stock doesn't meet your growth expectations you have spent money for the right to buy a stock at perhaps a higher price than it's selling for. As with any leveraged position, you accelerate your risk.

12. OPTIONS: Futures options are like stock options in that they determine, before the fact, the price of your anticipated purchase. In the futures market this means you have preset your total loss exposure.

13. FUTURES TRADING: Futures trading involves commodities, index futures, foreign currency, etc. Futures trading is extremely volatile, and, perhaps more important, you can lose substantially more than you have invested.

I am sure you noted that this listing would be directly inverted if you were to list the investments in the order of their potential rewards. For example, futures trading can make you rich in a rather short period of time. However, it more likely will make you poor. On the other hand, while time certificates of deposit are safe, they offer little in return. For most, a middle-ground approach will be best: a good return with a moderate element of risk.

Safety should not be the sole determining factor in your investment vehicle choice. However, it must be an important consideration, which explains my elaboration.

Unfortunately many investors are confused. They want to create their fortune with investments better suited for the purpose of continuing wealth than for acquiring it, or they use short-term vehicles to achieve long-term goals. That confusion can be overcome. Coupled with these lists indicating strong and weak points of certain investments, the next chapter will help you make your investment vehicle decisions. But before we turn to the specifics of certain investments, you should be reminded of the obvious: I'm not presenting every possibility. There are many unorthodox investment opportunities (like personal lending). And nontraditional choices may be your best option. Don't ignore any possibility. The Rational Investor principle works with any investment vehicle. All you need to do is keep in mind the general criteria discussed in this chapter.

5

The Best Investment?

Most investors have no idea what a given investment has returned historically. For example, do you know what rank silver has for its general investment returns over the last fifteen years? Ask yourself the same question for gold, bonds, real estate, investment stamps, or the stock market. If you don't know, how could you make an intelligent financial decision in any of those areas of investment or speculation? The answer is: you couldn't. If you did invest without that information, you invested unwisely. You accepted an unnecessary level of risk.

Although an investment can exceed, or fall short of, the historical norms, over a period of time the returns will average out. Even if you exceed accepted standards at every turn you still have limits. Let's say you do better than most investors in a given field by 50 percent, which is highly unlikely. If the norm were a return of 6 percent, you would only increase your gross by 3 percentage points for a total of 9 percent. That's not enough. In fact, it may be almost impossible to receive the kind of returns you need to acquire wealth using many standard investment vehicles. The information in the following list should give you some indications of relative performance.

THE BEST INVESTMENT BY RATE RETURN:

1.	INVESTMENT QUALITY U.S. COINS	18%
2.	GOLD	15%
3.	INVESTMENT QUALITY STAMPS	14%
4.	OIL	13%
5.	DIAMONDS	10%
6.	STOCKS	10%
7.	BONDS	9%
8.	TREASURY BILLS	8%
9.	SILVER	8%
10.	REAL ESTATE	8%

These rates are based on a fifteen year average (1971 - 1985). Any meaningful comparison of historical data should cover as much time as possible. Also, the percentages in this list are rounded off to the nearest percent, which the item's position takes into account.

Does this information mean all readers should invest in U.S. coins? Of course not. They represent a tricky field of investment. Unless you're an expert, or employ one, you can lose your shirt along with your coins. But it does mean that maybe you should consider investment quality U.S. coins as a part of your investment plan. It's hard to ignore financial bottom lines, and this one says U.S. coins consistantly outperform traditional investments. Considering this kind of data dictates diversification in areas you probably never considered, but you need to gather further information before proceeding. Why? Because averaged listings are dangerous without specifics. For instance, the rate return for U.S. coins is usually consistent throughout the years. Gold is just the opposite, with large cyclical price swings. Although gold offers a good average return, it is volatile. If your entry timing is faulty, you stand to lose big. So don't rely too much on any listings, including mine. These only offer possibilities based on statistical data. As with all financial investment considerations, these findings have to be tailored to your needs to be effective.

I hope that some of you are surprised with the results of this survey. Specifically, I draw your attention to the fact that stocks finished sixth in those investments examined. They returned little more than half of the leader. That indicates that the stock market, for many the most traditional investment vehicle, needs to be drastically reevaluated. Its historical average return is small while offering potential substantial risks. Its risk/return ratio is suspect.

If ever there was an indication that diversification is necessary for safety and return results, this is it. If ever there was an indication that creative thinking is required for personal wealth, this is it. If ever there was an indication that brokers, bankers, and financial counselors are offering what's good for their bottom line as opposed to yours, this is it. Most of them offer hot stock tips, and the majority of those turn out to be losers. When's the last time your broker recommended investment quality coins as a part of your portfolio? How about stamps? The probable answer is never, because they don't sell coins or stamps. They sell only a small portion of what should be your many options. Unfortunately, most investors never expand their thinking beyond their broker's recommendations. That narrow outlook means they lose excellent investment opportunities that historically surpass the stock market. Look at it another way by answering this question: If during the Crash of '87 you had been diversified according to this listing, would you have been better off than most investors? You bet you would!

I bring this information to you so you can make informed decisions with your money. *An investor with limited funds and a financial education will ultimately be wealthy!* An investor with unlimited funds and little financial education will ultimately be poor. That's because the financial world plays hardball, and is designed to penalize those that don't understand the system. Those that do, profit.

The best investment? In a general sense it doesn't matter. What's important is your best investment, and only you can decide that. The one thing I'm sure of after looking at the previous chapter and this survey, is that it's probably not what you thought it was. Don't get fooled or caught up in what everyone else is doing. Forget the experts that, if the truth be told, are wrong far, far more often than they are right. Look at the facts. Then choose investment vehicles that will be part of your Rational Investing plan. All financially successful people employ this hands-on approach.

WHAT YOUR INVESTMENTS ACTUALLY PRODUCE

Most of us, when reviewing an investment opportunity, look for the best interest rate or return. Little else is considered. For instance, if bank X has a 10 percent interest rate for their two year TCD, and bank Y offers 10.5 percent for the same certificate, we invest with bank Y. Very few bother to ascertain how both banks arrive at their interest rate; i.e., what method of interest computation do they use? Without that vital piece of information we don't have the facts that allow for an intelligent decision. This holds true for the more sophisticated investments as well.

As hard as this may be for you to believe, it is possible that bank X has the best interest rate return. How? For the sake of argument let's say that bank X uses day-of-deposit-to-day-of-withdrawal/compounded and paid daily interest. Bank Y is on FIFO (First In/First Out), compounded and paid quarterly. Further, let's assume they

have a full-quarter requirement on all deposits, which
means all monies have to be on deposit for the full 90
days to receive interest. Many banks have this requisite.

It should be immediately obvious that daily interest is
better than quarterly interest as your interest starts compounding interest that much faster. Also, bank X gives
you flexibility because no matter when you make a withdrawal, you will have received interest for the entire time
the bank used your money.

Bank Y, on the other hand, even though they offered a
higher rate, would only pay you interest provided you
leave the monies on deposit the full quarter. If you make
a withdrawal on the 75th day, you lose 75 days worth of
interest.

There are more important considerations. Let's go further, and look at an example account at bank Y to make
the point.

Balance on 1st day of quarter	$5,000
Deposit on 15th day of quarter	2,500
Balance to date	7,500
Deposit on 30th day of quarter	7,000
Balance to date	14,500
Withdrawal on 60th day of quarter	2,500
Balance to date	12,000
Withdrawal on 80th day of quarter	3,000
Balance to date	9,000
Deposit on 87th day of quarter	3,000
Balance on last day of quarter	12,000

Now, assuming our example interest rate of 10.5 percent for bank Y, what do you believe would be the interest
earned during the quarter? Bank Y, with its half a percentage point higher interest rate than bank X will pay
the customer no interest for the quarter. That's because
all of the deposits will earn nothing, as they will not meet
the full-quarter requirement, and the original balance of

five thousand dollars will also lose its interest as, using the First In/First Out method, all withdrawals during the quarter come out of that balance. Pretty simple, isn't it. Thousands, perhaps millions, of bank customers earn nothing on their savings because they are not aware that banks are allowed to use varying methods of computing interest.

In this example the immediate point is that to compare rates you have to ensure that both institutions are using the same method of interest computation. Only at that point is rate shopping possible. All things are not what they seem in the financial world, even in something as simple as a savings account. Think about what you are up against with some of the more complicated vehicles.

With this in mind, let's consider what rate of savings interest you need just to maintain the status quo. As of this writing, inflation is at 4.5 percent. Most of us believe this indicates that you have to have an interest rate of at least 4.5 percent to break even. What we are forgetting is the tax consideration. If you're in the 28 percent bracket, you need substantial additional interest. Look at the following example:

Regular savings balance	$1,000.00
Interest rate	5.5%
Interest earned	+$55.00
Minus inflationary loss of $1,000.00 at 4.5%	-$45.00
Minus tax on interest earned at 28%	-$15.40
Profit or (Loss)	($5.40)

For this account to have the purchasing power of a year ago you needed an interest rate of 6.26 percent. They only paid 5.5 percent. Clearly, under many market conditions, most bank accounts don't produce the required profits. They would have to improve their rates dramatically just to get to a break-even point, and even that would be unacceptable. You shouldn't be investing to break even.

Regrettably, even in the best of times, many investments run backwards. Imagine the impact of rampant inflation. That narrows the field even further. It is imperative that you consider all pertinent information in your investment choices.

Specifically:

1. When and if you compare rates, make sure you are comparing likes that allow for such a comparison.

2. After arriving at your choice apply other applicable considerations, such as the inflation rate and taxes. Then see if the choice still makes sense.

Rational Investing does it all if you will allow it. But, you have to ignore most accepted standards and understand how the game is played. Comprehending the nuances of certain vehicles is an important cog in that thought process. As I have said, the plan will work regardless of your level of expertise, but why settle for less when you could have more?

One final note: as you can see from my example about banks, you should never trust anyone with your finances, even someone as apparently harmless as your "friendly" local banker. Like any sales representative, bankers too will take as much of your money as they can, and they do so by contriving circumstances you can't control or easily understand. Unfortunately, that's how most people in the financial marketplace make their money. You don't need to be paranoid, but a sceptical perspective won't hurt. With Rational Investing you won't have to trust anyone, including me, to have dependable, profitable results.

You must consider every investment opportunity. Then dissect every facet of that specific vehicle. No stone should be unturned, no prospect ignored.

The Twelve Percent
Investment Rule

After my warning against generic investment advice, you might be surprised to see the word "rule" in the title of this chapter. But you may also have been wondering how to choose the best time to be in a particular investment. This chapter provides a guide for investment timing that by itself can make you an overall winner. It's called the Twelve Percent Investment Rule.

Researching investors that have shown a track record of profitability sent me in a direction I didn't expect. It soon became obvious that as profitable as their portfolios may have been, their return could have been better. These investors were all missing one important, if not critical, ingredient. No matter what the trade or investment, they missed the best moment to buy or sell. Even successful investors are constantly saying things like, "I made money, but I wish I had sold three weeks ago." Translated, this means, "I made a bundle, but I could have made more." That's what happens when you try to decipher the market rather than having a preordained plan. Even your winners can be disappointing.

You cannot foretell the future, so you will always be faced with the possibility of losing a portion of your profit. The Twelve Percent Investment Rule can protect your profits almost entirely. It works for all investment portfolios. It doesn't matter if you have $250,000 in stocks, $5,000 in mutual funds, or $2,000 in a TCD at your local bank. The rule is based on economic history, which states: the economy is inconsistantly cyclical. It should be obvious that if you use only one investment vehicle you will be the victim of forces that will have little to do with your investment choice. If you always invest with your bank, you will sometimes receive a high savings rate, sometimes a low rate. You will be able to react only to outside forces, and therefore won't be able to control the bottom-line results. Ideally you want to be in a position to act rather than react. Timing is the key. This is true for the stock market, commodities, real estate— all forms of investments. It even holds true for what is generally a family's largest investment— their house.

The point is that to maximize your net return on your risk capital, you have to have a plan that immediately sees changes in the economy, and therefore increases your profitable opportunities. You want to be liquid when money markets are paying 16 percent and in the stock market when it's on its way to the moon. Unfortunately, most are usually in the opposite position. Even you winners out there would have to admit that you get whipsawed once or twice a year due to forces outside of your control. In either case, missing the vital sign in terms of timing either cost you some of your profit or your capital. There must be some way to lessen the negative impact of this investment fact of life. That's the purpose of the Twelve Percent Investment Rule.

The rule is very simple: when the prime interest rate is below 12 percent, you should be in the stock market; when it rises to 12 percent and above, you should be into money markets, bonds, etc. That's it. Remember, this is a portfolio rule, not one for individual trades. In fact, the rule is nothing more than a commonsense rationale or deduction about how financial markets behave. It doesn't force a balance; rather, it looks at all aspects, especially economic history, and draws an all-encompassing conclusion that stands inspection at any level. Pick a day in time, apply the rule, and see if your bottom-line investment results would not have been improved if you had acted on this very basic timing sign. The rule continually substantiates itself.

There is nothing fancy here, and I hope its simplicity doesn't offend your investment IQ. It shouldn't, but some people prefer charts, graphs, and verbiage to results. There are thousands of investment experts out there who produce nothing but profits for themselves at the expense of their clients. You get tons of financial fluff: charts, investment doublespeak, folders, and a hot-line phone number. What you don't get is large profits following their advice.

You will be hard pressed to learn anything more valuable than the Twelve Percent Investment Rule. It reduces the subjectivity of your educated guesses. Again, specific investments are left to you, but now you have a timing response mechanism. After all, investing is, at a minimum a two-step proposition: First, what is the market doing? Second, what vehicle am I going to invest in under these conditions?

Most investors only consider the vehicle. Even those of you who do consider the larger market picture usually leave that decision to the subjective opinion of your adviser or broker which can be a catastrophic mistake. As I mention throughout this book, their interests are not concurrent with your financial well-being. They make money whether you do or not, and regardless of what they tell you, they are paid for their volume of sales not client results.

It should be noted that you can fine tune the Twelve Percent Investment Rule to meet your needs. Obviously prime doesn't have to be exactly 12 percent to make a move one way or the other. Clear up or down movements indicating that the percentage will be reached should be acted on before the fact. The moment you're convinced of the trend, act on its implications. Let the rate, and what it represents, make its own statement. One thing you mustn't do is ignore what it tells you. That will be costly in the long run. Remember, the more variables you can remove from your investment program, the more successful it will become. The Twelve Percent Investment Rule helps accomplish that goal.

Why, you may ask, does the rule work? Most of you realize the beauty of its simple, unstated conclusion. Ignore all the peripheral, extraneous data usually put forth as investment advice and you are left with the undeniable fact that when interest rates (prime, as understood by most) are moving up over 12 percent, the markets are usually in the overall process of retreating. The reverse is also true. Once prime moves below 12 percent the market is usually making sizable advances. I caution that the Twelve Percent Investment Rule will have no immediate impact or repercussion regarding a specific investment you may have. It will simply set in motion the proper response to events as they unfold—events most will not decipher until it's too late and they have to pay a perhaps exorbitant price for their tardiness.

If you are able to act on these constantly occurring swings, you will be better able to limit your losses and increase your gains. Again, the rule works with little or no guesswork.

The rule is flexible, which is a very important aspect of any profitable investment plan. It tells you where to invest, and it tells you when. What to invest in is left to your requirements, expectations, and needs. Again, invest in the market when prime is below 12 percent and in money markets when it's over 12 percent.

If you read no further, this rule will help your investments, and it can be used in any and all situations. However, the rule is only a small part of the Rational Investing plan. You understand the rule. You understand how it works and what it represents. The Twelve Percent Investment Rule takes advantage of prime's representational value. It allows the plan to better serve your needs by choosing a more profitable liquidity position as events dictate.

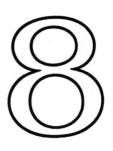

The Ten Commandments of Stock Market Success

I hope you realize by now that the stock market is no place for amateurs.

Yet, in terms of numerical volume, amateurs form the largest group in the market. That's why the insiders, brokers, and floor traders fare so well. They have easy pickings.

Typical investors are likely either to rely solely on their brokers, a dangerous error, or to be entirely on their own. The latter kind is often a compulsive gambler type who, instead of going to Vegas, turns to the market for a daily thrill fix. This person is usually overinvested, loves to trade on the latest rumor or hot tip, and is unhappy when nothing is happening. He or she will even sell out a long-term winner just to make a trade.

It doesn't matter what your problem with the market is, you first have to admit you have one and then work to correct it. How do you know if you've even got a problem? Look at your track record. Are you consistently making a profit or not? After expenses, are you making money, and at what rate? If you're only returning, as an example, 5 to 10 percent net on your market investments, I'd suggest you get out immediately. The reasoning is simple: you're risking 100 percent of your investment capital for a paltry return. In fact, as mentioned earlier, those returns can be surpassed with investment coins, real estate, or personal lending, where your element of risk is lessened.

The stock market gives many a false picture of what the risk and rewards actually are. There are four categories of market players: the big winners, the small winners, the small losers, and the big losers. The big winners are the Wall Street traders. The small winners are the broker types, and a small portion of the individual investors. The small losers are the individual traders. The big losers are the complusive individual traders. In the end, only the professionals win.

However, as the saying goes, a high tide raises all boats. So, in a strong bull market all positions tend to improve greatly. There is nothing wrong with taking advantage of that fact. However, most individual traders will give back all their winnings when the market turns around. That was proven in the Crash of '87. The amateurs can only consistantly win in a no-lose situation. The pros win all the time. So don't allow success in the best of times to cloud your thinking.

Nevertheless, the stock market has certain undeniable advantages. It's easy to get into, and trading costs can be quite low if you use a discount broker. There's a wealth of substantial information available (I'm not talking about hot-tip newsletters) at any local library, the financial pages of your newspaper, and through many radio and television shows. And the returns can be substantial.

Regardless of the amount and quality of your reference information, to be profitable in the stock market, you need a set of rules that you follow religiously. Here are "The Ten Commandments":

1. NEVER TRADE MORE THAN 10 PERCENT OF YOUR CAPITAL ON ONE TRADE. This will stop you from ever overtrading. This pertains to your personal investment decisions. Rational Investing, as explained later, occasionally acts contrary to this rule.

2. DIVERSIFY. Trade five to ten stocks or mutual funds.

3. USE STOP-LOSS ORDERS IN SOME FORM. Always protect your capital, profits, and individual trades. Rational Investing does this for you.

4. TRADE ONLY ACTIVE STOCKS. Buying inactive issues is like being trapped in quicksand.

5. A GRAIN OF DOUBT IS A MOUNTAIN OF TROUBLE. Whether it's the market in its entirety or a specific issue, if you've got any doubt, pass. You don't have to trade all the time. In fact, there are times when you should be out of the market altogether. It's hard sometimes, but a move based on anxiousness is almost always a big loser. That's why Rational Investing removes you from the equation as much as possible.

6. THE BULL ISN'T THE ONLY WINNER. As mentioned above, everyone can win in a long-term bull market. The real test comes when the bear arrives. Winners make money because they understand and can profit from both sides of the equation. If all you know is how to buy, you've got problems. They may not be apparent right now, but they will be. Here again, if you're using Rational Investing, this is done for you;

i.e., YOU PROFIT IN ANY MARKET. Very few people can say the same thing.

7. UNDERSTAND WHY YOU'RE BUYING. It's important, regardless of your position and holdings, that you purchase shares for the right reason.

8. DON'T HEDGE AS A GENERAL INVESTMENT TECH-NIQUE. There are times when it is appropriate, but those are rare. If you feel the need to hedge (which can drastically reduce your potential profit), you should reexamine the investment.

9. DON'T PYRAMID. The average investor is not emo-tionally or financially equipped to take the added risk of using margins. I know many have used this tech-nique profitably, but for every one winner there are thousands of losers. The corresponding risk is not acceptable.

10. RETAIN AN ORIGINAL 10 PERCENT LIQUID CAPITAL ACCOUNT. Add to it with every winning trade. As corny as a rainy-day position may sound, when it all hits the fan, you'll be glad you thought ahead. It may mean the difference between having to accept a total loss or being able to hang in there. Think of it as your market/investment insurance policy. Here again, Ra-tional Investing takes this into account, as you will see.

These rules can be applied to any investment or invest-ment plan. They can make you a steady winner. Used with the other programs and techniques I've outlined, they take on added importance.

Again, the market is no place for amateurs. *The "Ten Commandments" in this chapter are important steps in helping make you a pro.* But that's not the only reason I laid them out. I explained them so you can see how and why Rational Investing works. The commandments will either help you make your investment vehicle choice or they are built into the plan. They should greatly increase your market knowledge and confidence.

Market Benchmarks

The stock market is rigged. I state again, because of its importance: professionals win; most individual investors lose. That's a reality that must be understood and then defeated.

If the market actually reflected true corporate worth, the Crash of '87 would not have occurred. Book value of stock didn't change from one day to the next. What changed was the rejection of overvaluation. And that means the stock market has no real accounting-based worth. It's all perception once book value is eclipsed by sale price. That float, the difference between corporate stock reality and market fantasy, allows manipulation of the market for the aggrandizement of the insiders (both individual and corporate). Their profit, of course, is arrived at by taking from the uninformed.

Now before you say that the pros lost in the Crash too, I remind you that they experienced the result of their own excesses. They weren't market victims, *They were the cause of the crash!* They produced the overvaluation in the first place. They profited many times over by the overvaluation, and they did so for many years. They profited in commissions and trades. Their losses were minimal compared to their previous gains. Additionally, many of the consequences of Black Monday were triggered by the trading methods many pros still employ. Then too, they got out long before their individual clients were afforded that luxury. Events continue to make clear the undeniable fact that many investment markets are, in fact, rigged. Those that refuse to believe that are an investment accident looking for a place to happen.

To explain further, let's look at an example. If the stock market were a true reflection of corporate America you would have to admit that stock value in a stable, profitable corporation should not have been adversely affected by the Crash, yet all stock was. Why? Because the market has little to do with reality. Again, it's perception. Much of the stock available on the market is so severely overvalued and manipulated that stock having a book value of as little as a quarter is selling for three and four dollars. That leaves one with the startling bottom line that stock price has no basis in hard-value accounting analysis. The selling price of an individual stock is all too often the result of broker salesmanship as opposed to actual monetary value. The truth is many brokers and their houses are far worse than the most despicable used car salesman. Certainly, they're more economically dangerous.

That brings us to the fact that all stocks, regardless, are pawns of the market. When you invest in the market, you are making a system bet. Granted, the stock is important, and its impact on your net results cannot be ignored. But, more important in the total equation is the market and its direction. That brings us to the topic at hand: four specific benchmarks that will help you determine where the market is headed, which thereafter assist you in making winning investment vehicle choices.

The market, being so susceptible to manipulation and rumor, is quite often influenced by unrelated events. Conversely, many events are a reflection of the market. I believe, that among other things, you should be aware of certain indicators, *not because they are actually important, but rather because the market thinks they are important.* These benchmarks are:

1. EMPLOYMENT TRENDS: Movement in the number of jobs created each month gives an indication that the economy is strong or retreating. Sustained growth is perhaps the best indication of an economy showing bullish trends, whereas the opposite indicates a possible market retreat, since employment figures affect so many variables that influence markets in general. For instance, fewer jobs mean more unemployment claims, less tax income, and reduced consumer spending.

2. CONSUMER SPENDING: Obviously, this is to be coupled with the preceding benchmark to see the full impact of current events. Here we have a measure of consumer confidence; although, there are times, around Christmas for instance, when the figures' importance are to be tempered. However, consumer spending influences all aspects of business and, as such, helps management make decisions regarding the future, both short and long term.

3. PERSONAL INCOME: It should be obvious that if personal income is rising, the economy appears strong. The reverse is also true. I caution, however, that personal income statistics, to have investment direction value, have to be used in conjunction with

known information regarding inflation. You need to see a net effect; i.e., we know inflation can drive personal income higher, but at the same time personal spending power may have decreased.

4. THE CONSUMER PRICE INDEX: Interest rates are affected by inflation, as you know. The Consumer Price Index (CPI) can help give you an indication of the direction interest rates will be driven— a powerful cue when coupled with The Twelve Percent Investment Rule. It also gives an indication of what business borrowing will be, which affects manufacturing, etc.

The overall economy is affected by many circumstances, some controlled, like the money supply, and some uncontrolled, like events in the Middle East. That means that, regardless of one's accuracy in predicting events, there is an implied element of risk with even the safest investments and substantially more with any speculation. Yet, if you understand the overall market concept, as opposed to just individual investment vehicle choice considerations, your win/loss ratio will improve dramatically. Stocks, gold, collectibles, real estate— they are all affected by the economy.

You must constantly review certain market benchmarks. They have perception merit, which is why I bring them to your attention. Spend more time studying the market in a total economic sense. As much as possible, stop listening to your broker or anyone when they tout specific stocks. *In a most consequential way, the market moves individual investments; individual investments don't move the market.* Most investors don't understand that principle, which is why they are disappointed in their results.

10

Mutual Funds

Mutual funds offer the investor so many advantages over individual stocks or other investments that they demand attention and consideration from every investor.

That statement is true in the best of times, and even more so now that we have such a capricious economy. Banks are in trouble, the stock market has experienced the Crash of '87, inflation is always a threat, increases in our personal taxes are in the works, the FSLIC is bankrupt, and so on. We are on a rollercoaster ride that may cost many of the uninformed more than they are willing to spend. The bill for the failure of government and our supposedly free market is always paid for by the middle class, and there will be no exception in the future.

Yet, even in the worst of times there is money to be made. What's more, you have no choice. Investing is not open to discussion. No matter what your financial station in life, you have to invest to cement the present and secure the future.

So we are presented with a problem. We have to invest and yet the market is rigged. Cracking the market's codes is a full-time job.

In earlier chapters I explained investment techniques that will give you direction in your investment choices. But even if you do choose that right area to invest, you can still lose if you choose the wrong broker, company, or commodity. If you're good, or lucky, you'll still be wrong the preponderance of the time. Don't let that bother you. Most experts are too. They live on their few successes and forget their voluminous failures. Unfortunately, most of us can't afford to play that game because we are playing with our own money. They're not. We have to beat the odds, and mutual funds can help.

Mutual funds offer the chance to exercise your investment choice (for instance, growth funds, precious metals funds, high-tech funds, medical funds, etc.) while you have the security of employing an expert who has something to lose. That's a very different relationship than the one you have with a broker. Funds allow you to use your common sense and apply certain Rational Investing rules to move your money as changes in the economy dictate. More specifically, mutual funds offer the following:

1. LOW RISK: Mutual funds are highly regulated. They provide relative safety within the confines of an investment field. For example, a health service mutual fund might get out of company X because they have management or cash flow problems. If you were invested in that stock, as opposed to a fund that had a portion of its money in the company, you would more than likely lose money, whereas the fund will cushion or negate the reversal. Risk is further decreased because fund managers with bad results don't last long (again, as opposed to a straight broker), which means they have a vested interest in results, not just sales commissions.

2. DIVERSIFICATION: This is especially helpful to the smaller investor. A fund can give you access to a number of stocks, etc., that by yourself you might not be able to afford. Current law says a fund cannot have more than 5 percent of its assets in any one company, which forces diversification and added safety.

3. LOW OR NO COST (Fees): Mutual fund shares have the commission included in the shares, and they have no fee whatsoever. They also allow for fractional shares, which, again, is important for the smaller investor. This feature works well with Rational Investing. (Note: Some funds do have fees, but we try to avoid those companies because they reduce our net.)

4. LIQUIDITY: Mutual funds are almost as liquid as cash. Certainly, they are more liquid than a bank time, certificate of deposit, and, in fact, can be turned around faster than most stock transactions.

5. LOW MINIMUMS: Most funds allow entry for as little as one thousand dollars and transactions of fifty to one hundred dollars. Nowhere else can you invest for these kinds of returns with so little to start.

6. CONSTANT PROFESSIONAL MANAGEMENT: As I mentioned earlier, you have to be a professional or employ one. A mutual fund relationship allows for that necessary financial expertise.

7. FLEXIBILITY: Most funds have a parallel money market account for their customers. When circumstances indicate a return to cash investments (following the Twelve Percent Investment Rule), you don't have to make any adjustments or pay additional fees. All you have to do is make a phone call, usually toll free, and transfer the amount you think prudent. The interest rates on mutual funds' money market accounts are

very competitive, and usually exceed what banks offer.

8. PROFITS IN BULL OR BEAR MARKETS: Most funds have a number of different funds that offer varying specialities. That variety means you can shift from yesterday's hot stocks to what's hot now.

9. EASY ACCESS TO PERFORMANCE DATA: You can quickly find out how mutual funds have performed in the past. As a guide to choosing a good one, companies themselves publish their historical performance (when they're good, of course). Additionally, financial and consumer publications track all major funds. Compare that with the difficulty you'd have trying to find out your broker's track record.

What's the rate of return on mutual funds? Historically, they beat all comers. You have to be careful when comparing investments since, as previously reviewed, the basis of comparison can give a false impression. That's why a specific percentage isn't noted. However, even with the safety factor that the market doesn't offer, mutual funds historically beat the Dow-Jones in averaged returns. Because funds are diversified and have differing objectives, you are better served verifying a specific fund's record, as opposed to that of the industry.

Mutual funds are unique investment tools. Their returns are more than competitive, with a fraction of the risk offered by most investment vehicles. They are more flexible, diversified, and liquid too. In addition, they cost little or nothing to purchase.

I have always been pleased with the results of mutual fund investments. That's even more true now that we have a market teetering on turmoil. Of course, the ultimate responsibility rests with you. Just because you invest in mutual funds doesn't mean you won't be hurt when and if the market corrects itself. At that point you have to be in the right mutual fund, which my nonplan investment advice and techniques should help you accomplish.

What follows is a brief listing of some of the more successful funds in various areas of the market. It should give you an idea of the range of possibilities that mutual funds offer. Don't look upon it as final or fixed in any way, just as a few places to start your inquiries. These are not specific fund recommendations.

Mutual Funds Listing

Aggressive Growth Funds:

>   Twentieth Century Vista 1–800–345–2021
>   Janus 1–800–525–3713

Government Securities Funds:

>   Freedom Gold & Government Trust
>   1–800–225–6713
>   Scudder Government Mortgage Securities Fund
>   1–800–225–2470

Long-Term Growth Funds:

>   Alger Small Capitalization 1–800–992–3863
>   GT America Growth 1–800–824–1580

Balanced Funds:

>   Axe-Houghton Fund B 1–800–431–1030
>   Wellington Fund 1–800–662–7447

Growth and Income Funds:

>   State Bond Common Stock 1–800–333–3952
>   Financial Industrial Income 1–800–525–8085

Corporate Bond Funds:

Dreyfus Strategic Income 1–800–648–9048
Bartlett Fixed Income 1–800–543–0863

Tax Free Bond Funds:

Steinroe High Yield Muni 1–800–338–2550
Pru-Bache Muni High Yield 1–800–225–1852

International Funds:

Van Eck World Income 1–800–221–2220
AMA Income-Global Short Term
    1–800–262– 3863.

Precious Metals Funds:

USAA Gold Fund 1–800–531–8000
US New Prospector 1–800–824–4653

Sector Funds:

Financial Strategic Health & Sciences Portfolio
    1–800–525–8085
Vanguard Specialized Portfolio Energy
    1–800–662–7447

Complete detailed listings for most successful funds are available in *Money* or *Changing Times*.

Mutual funds have unlimited potential for your Rational Investor plan. For most readers they are the best investment vehicle for the program, which is why I so highly recommend them. They cover all investment fields. It's up to you to pick one right for you. But no matter what mutual fund you choose, your return should be more than adequate to allow Rational Investing to produce the wealth you deserve.

PART III

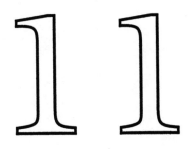

The Plan and How It Works

I have already mentioned a number of the components that go into Rational Investing and your investment vehicle choice. I did that so you would get a feel for what this program is all about. I also wanted you to realize that, as simple as this plan is, it is well thought out and researched. The percentages used in the plan's formula have been carefully weighted for the best results.

Most important, I realized that I had to completely remove the subjectivity of the investor. Even the most objective among us have some preconceived notions and ideas about investments. That couldn't be allowed in the technical workings of the plan. Your preferences are only necessary when you choose the investment vehicle, and for that I have offered much to guide you. Even though subjectivity is involved, you and you alone are in the best position to decide what vehicles will meet your objectives and expectations.

My father once told me that everything in the universe, excluding human nature and personality traits, could be expressed somehow in numbers and then used in that form to solve the problem at hand. Simply stated, he meant that by reducing things to the most easily understood numerical equation and then letting the numbers speak, you could remove the possibility of human error. In other words, find the formula and you've found the answer. Use the answer, in the form of the formula, and you have the ability to outperform the norms. In this case that means profits.

Being a financial professional, I obviously use numbers. I found that they can be most enlightening. Assuming the integrity of the presenter, numbers don't lie. They offer what mere words can't. They can offer direction. They can identify problems. They can solve problems. Now, before you get the idea that I am solely a number cruncher, let me tell you that nothing could be further from the truth. I believe in individuals first, their numbers second. However, when reviewing the investment field I realized that I had to devise a plan that would, by relying entirely on numbers, negate the investor's tendency to make mistakes.

Let's get started.

All you will need is a ten-column, columnar pad (you'll use only nine columns), which all stationery stores carry. They're a couple of dollars.

You will want to make your nine column headings as follows:

1. UNIT PRICE: This means exactly what it says: the amount that represents the value, or price, of one unit of investment in your plan. That can be the price of one unit of a mutual fund, one share of stock, one gold coin, etc. This UNIT PRICE will change as the value of one unit of your investment increases or decreases. The first entry on your sheet, under UNIT

PRICE, will be your ENTRY LEVEL PRICE, or, the unit price you initially paid. We will use it later.

2. PORTFOLIO VALUE: This represents the total cash value of your investment choice at any given time. You arrive at it by multiplying the UNIT PRICE by the UNITS OWNED column.

3. CASH: Just as it says, this column represents the total of your CASH. At the start of the program CASH is 50 percent of the TOTAL INVESTMENT VALUE (as is PORTFOLIO VALUE) and then is adjusted accordingly as we progress.

4. UNITS BOUGHT (SOLD): This represents the number of units bought or (sold) as directed by the MANAGE-MENT APPLICATION INSTRUCTIONS (as outlined in Tables 3 and 4). It allows you to keep track of your monthly transactions.

5. UNITS OWNED: The number of total units owned at any given time. It is constantly changing as purchases and sales are completed.

6. MANAGEMENT APPLICATION (BUY or SELL as out-lined in Tables 3 and 4): The heart of the plan. The MANAGEMENT APPLICATION gives you the direction to make purchases and sales. It is the only real calculation you have to make. Others are simply a reflection of what the MANAGEMENT APPLICATION calculation did to other areas. This MANAGEMENT APPLICATION calculation, the most important task you have to perform, takes approximately two min-utes.

7. BOUGHT (SOLD) $ AMOUNT: This represents, in dol-lars, the value of your purchases and sales. It is then used to calculate your UNITS BOUGHT (SOLD), which is then used to adjust your UNITS OWNED column.

8.   INTEREST: This is the interest amount you are earning with your CASH in the program. Remember, CASH is an asset, and you want a return that helps the plan's bottom line.

9.   TOTAL INVESTMENT VALUE: This is the total value of your Rational Investing plan. It is the sum of your PORTFOLIO VALUE and CASH columns.

To get started, let's use an example program.

The first entry (on Table 5) indicates a $10,000 total investment value, which is nothing more than an example figure. All other figures are based on the percentages and figures as dictated by the management application. Let's go over the first entry column by column.

1.   The UNIT PRICE (also your ENTRY LEVEL PRICE from now on), is the cost of one unit of the investment vehicle.

2.   The PORTFOLIO VALUE is 50 percent of your TOTAL INVESTMENT VALUE.

3.   The CASH is 50 percent of your TOTAL INVESTMENT VALUE. In subsequent months you will add to this column your interest earned and subtract the amount of any purchases the MANAGEMENT APPLICATION directs you to buy.

4.   The UNITS BOUGHT (SOLD) is your PORTFOLIO VALUE divided by the UNIT PRICE. Later this is determined by the MANAGEMENT APPLICATION.

5.   The UNITS OWNED represents the total units, which at this point is nothing more than your original purchase.

6.   The MANAGEMENT APPLICATION may be thought of as the percentage of your portfolio you should buy or sell. In the case of our first entry, the UNIT PRICE of

$10.00 minus the UNIT PRICE of $8.00 (the second month's UNIT PRICE) divided by the ENTRY LEVEL PRICE ($10.00) and then divided by the WEIGHT FACTOR of four. For a complete explanation of the MANAGEMENT APPLICATION I refer you to Tables 3 and 4.

7. BOUGHT (SOLD) $ AMOUNT is how much money the MANAGEMENT APPLICATION directs you to buy or sell.

8. The INTEREST (for this example we are using a 10 percent rate) is your CASH figure times .10 divided by 12 (since every line represents a month).

9. The TOTAL INVESTMENT VALUE is your PORTFOLIO VALUE plus your CASH value.

You can take any line of this example and see how I arrived at these figures.

Let me explain the all-important management application in detail. If the unit price has gone up, you sell. If the unit price has gone down, you buy. The amount of a buy or sell order is tied to your entry level price (the unit price at the time of your original investment) since all your investment decisions should be predicated on your buy-in price. Look at Table 3. It shows the simple formula for monthly managment application decisions. There are only four possibilities.

The weight factor chart (Table 4) gives you the final figure in the management application formula. It works like this. If the unit price is above your entry level price, subtract your entry levl price from the unit price. Divide that answer by the entry level price. Then find that figure's range on the chart. It gives you the weight factor for the management application. For example: If your unit price was $5.00 and going up, and your entry level price was $3.50, you'd subtract $3.50 from $5.00. Then divide the

TABLE 3
Management Application

	Monthly Price Goes Up	Monthly Price Goes Down
	SELL INSTRUCTIONS	**BUY INSTRUCTIONS**
UNIT PRICE above ENTRY LEVEL PRICE	Current UNIT PRICE minus your ENTRY LEVEL PRICE equals X. X divided by your ENTRY LEVEL PRICE equals Y. Y is then divided by the WEIGHT FACTOR. Multiply the answer by PORTFOLIO VALUE. This gives you the dollar amount to SELL.	Current UNIT PRICE minus your ENTRY LEVEL PRICE equals X. X divided by your ENTRY LEVEL PRICE equals Y. Y is then divided by the WEIGHT FACTOR. Multiply the answer by previous month's CASH value. This gives you the dollar amount to BUY.
UNIT PRICE below ENTRY LEVEL PRICE	The ENTRY LEVEL PRICE minus the current UNIT PRICE equals X. X divided by your ENTRY LEVEL PRICE equals Y. Y is then divided by the WEIGHT FACTOR. Multiply the answer by PORTFOLIO VALUE. This gives you the dollar amount to SELL.	Your ENTRY LEVEL PRICE minus the current UNIT PRICE equals X. X divided by your ENTRY LEVEL PRICE equals Y. Y is then divided by the WEIGHT FACTOR. Multiply the answer by previous month's CASH value. This gives you the dollar amount to BUY.

TABLE 4
How to Compute the Weight Factor

	Weight Factor	
Y^a (%)	Monthly Price Goes Up (SELL	Monthly Price Goes Down (BUY)
UNIT PRICE above ENTRY LEVEL PRICE		
40.1 +	1	X^b
30.1 – 40.0	2	2
20.1 – 30.0	3	3
10.1 – 20.0	4	4
0.0 – 10.0	5	5
UNIT PRICE below ENTRY LEVEL PRICE		
0.0 – 10.0	5	5
10.1 – 20.0	4	4
20.1 – 30.0	3	3
30.1 – 40.0	2	2
40.1 +	X^b	1

[a] Y is taken from the Management Application. See Table 3.

[b] X represents a signal to do nothing. No matter what the unit price has done, you do not buy or sell.

TABLE 5
Rational Investor Example
(First Year)

Unit Price ($)	Portfolio Value ($)	Cash ($)	Units Bought (Sold)	Units Owned	Management Application	Bought (Sold) $ Amount	Interest ($)	Total Investment Value ($)
10	5,000	5,000	500.0	500.0	—	5,000	—	10,000
8	4,250	4,792	31.3	431.3	.05	250	42	9,042
7	4,198	4,353	68.4	599.7	.10	479	40	8,551
5	5,176	2,212	435.4	1,035.1	.50	2,177	36	7,388
4	5,468	903	331.8	1,366.9	.60	1,327	18	6,371
6	7,108	2,005	(182.3)	1,184.6	.20	(1,094)	8	9,113
8	9,122	2,377	(44.4)	1,140.2	.05	(355)	17	11,499
10	11,402	2,397	—	1,140.2	—	—	20	13,799
8	9,242	2,297	15.0	1,155.2	.05	120	20	11,539
5	6,925	1,167	229.8	1,385.0	.50	1,149	19	8,092
7	9,002	1,870	(99.0)	1,286.0	.10	(693)	10	10,872
8	9,838	2,336	(56.3)	1,229.7	.05	(450)	16	12,174

1. Unit price down 20%
2. Return from traditional investment technique— $2,000 Loss (-20% yield)
3. Return from saving $10,000 (at 10%)— $1,038.00 (10.38% yield)
4. Return with Rational Investing— $2,174.00 (21.7% yield)

TABLE 6
Rational Investor Example
(Second Year)

Unit Price ($)	Portfolio Value ($)	Cash ($)	Units Bought (Sold)	Units Owned	Management Application	Bought (Sold) $ Amount	Interest ($)	Total Investment Value ($)
10	12,297	2,356	—	1,229.7	—	—	20	14,653
9	11,114	2,329	5.2	1,234.9	.02	47	29	13,443
10	12,349	2,348	—	1,234.9	—	—	19	14,697
11	13,336	2,615	(22.5)	1,212.4	.02	(247)	20	15,951
12	13,882	3,304	(55.6)	1,156.8	.05	(667)	22	17,186
13	13,650	4,720	(106.8)	1,050.0	.10	(1,388)	28	18,370
14	11,970	7,489	(195.0)	855.0	.20	(2,730)	39	19,459
13	11,864	6,802	57.6	912.6	.10	749	62	18,666
15	7,757	12,791	(395.5)	517.1	.50	(5,932)	57	20,548
11	5,944	12,642	23.3	540.4	.02	256	107	18,586
9	5,117	12,494	28.1	568.5	.02	253	105	17,611
8	5,173	11,973	78.1	646.6	.05	625	104	17,146

1. Unit price down 20%
2. Return from traditional investment technique— $2,000 Loss (–10% ave. yield) (–20% total)
3. Return from saving $10,000 (at 10%)—$2,181 (10.9% ave. yield) (21.8% total)
4. Return with Rational Investing—$7,146 (35.8% ave. yield) (71.5% total)

TABLE 7
Rational Investor Example
(Third Year)

Unit Price ($)	Portfolio Value ($)	Cash ($)	Units Bought (Sold)	Units Owned	Management Application	Bought (Sold) $ Amount	Interest ($)	Total Investment Value ($)
9	5,717	12,176	(11.4)	635.2	.02	(103)	100	17,893
8	5,690	11,668	76.1	711.3	.05	609	101	17,358
7	6,146	10,598	166.7	878.0	.10	1,167	97	16,744
6	7,388	8,566	353.3	1,231.3	.20	2,120	88	15,954
7	7,880	9,376	(105.6)	1,125.7	.10	(739)	71	17,256
8	8,611	9,848	(49.3)	1,076.4	.05	(394)	78	18,459
9	9,516	10,102	(19.1)	1,057.3	.02	(172)	82	19,618
10	10,573	10,186	—	1,057.3	—	—	84	20,759
11	11,419	10,482	(19.2)	1,038.1	.02	(211)	85	21,901
12	11,886	11,139	(47.6)	990.5	.05	(571)	87	23,015
11	11,119	11,009	20.3	1,010.8	.02	223	93	22,128
10	10,108	11,101	—	1,010.8	—	—	92	21,209

1. Unit price is equal to original purchase price
2. Return from traditional investment technique— $.00 (0% ave. yield) (0% total)
3. Return from saving $10,000 (at 10%)— $3,443 (11.47% ave. yield) (34.4% total)
4. Return with Rational Investing— $11,209 (37.4% ave. yield) (112.1% total)

$1.50 answer by $3.50. The answer is .428, or 42.8 percent, which you divide by a weight factor of one. If the unit price is below your entry level price you simply reverse the procedure and subtract the unit price from the entry level price.

You can take any line from the example charts, and see exactly how I arrived at the numbers presented. You have only four choices and they're all outlined. There is a rarely used fifth direction. You do nothing if the unit price is the same from one month to the next and/or the entry level price and unit price are the same. Pick the one that applies and plug in your figures. The answer tells you exactly what dollar amount to buy or sell. When you buy, you apply the percentage to your cash. When you sell, you apply the percentage to your portfolio value. Both answers are then divided by the unit price to tell you how many units you have bought or sold. Every figure ties into another. All you have to do is ensure that your management application is correct.

The percentages represented by the four formulas are weighted for two reasons. The Rational Investor wants to force you into taking every opportunity to make money, while at the same time showing some restraint that will stop you from getting greedy. Greed in the market, as in every human endeavor, is the downfall of most (a subject reviewed in depth later). The plan removes or negates the greed factor as much as possible, always with the goal of making profit, even when it doesn't appear there is any to be made. Additionally, weighting accounts for cycles and what a price movement, up or down, represents.

Does Rational Investing work? Look at the results after each year. The normal investor, the guy that invests his $10,000 in company X and then sits back to wait for the money to come rolling in, ends up with $0. If he cashed out after the first year he would have lost $2,000, which, according to human nature, would have been most likely.

The saver type would have earned $1,038 (at the same 10 percent rate I used for our interest column). The saver continually earns money, but after inflation and taxes it's not much. In contrast, the plan made money each and every year. And it did so with an investment that went nowhere. In fact, the investment vehicle lost money the first year, but we didn't. We made money! After the second year the price was still below our entry level price, and even in the third year it only breaks even. No matter. Rational Investing made plenty. Over 37 percent (yearly average return) on an investment that, by itself, earned nothing. Not one red cent. Rational Investing makes money, as I've said before, by account management, timing, and valuating purchases and sales. Within reason, the investment vehicle doesn't matter. It can only make things better.

12

Questions and Answers

After reading the last chapter you're probably more than a little skeptical. I hope so. If anyone told me he had a plan that, under most circumstances, couldn't lose, I'd have some questions. Let me try to anticipate some of yours.

QUESTION 1:   Can I add money to the plan, and if so, how?

ANSWER: You can add money to the plan at any time. In fact, as I will outline in the chapter on savings, I strongly recommend it. Your capital should be constantly increasing, not only from the plan itself, but also from your income.

When adding to the plan, you only have to make one adjustment. First, whatever the amount, just like the original investment amount, it should be halved into cash and portfolio value. Next, you have to adjust your entry level price to reflect the added monies. Lets take our example again. Say you have another $2,000.00 you want to invest at the end of the first year. Fifty percent of that is $1,000.00. Put $1,000.00 in your cash account and buy $1,000.00 worth of units. The price at year end was $8.00 per unit, so you can buy another 125 units. Add the 125 units to your original number of units and you have 625. For that 625 units you spent $5,000.00 originally and $1,000.00 now. That's $6,000.00. Divide that by 625 and you have your new entry level price of $9.60. That is the figure you will use in place of the $10.00 that you were inserting in the formula whenever it called for entry level price. That figure will remain constant until you make another addition.

If your monthly additions to the plan are small, you may wish to adjust the entry level price quarterly, or even yearly. Use your judgment.

Remember, this entry level price is important. That is the benchmark that we will assess our results against.

QUESTION 2:   In your example you made use of the fact that the investment vehicle was very volatile. What happens if the investment vehicle doesn't move at all, up or down?

ANSWER: First of all, it should be noted that my example actually made a worst case scenario. The vehicle choice earned us nothing by itself. If the unit price had gone up over the three years, say to eighteen dollars, we would have done quite nicely. The point being that the example was, at the very least, fair.

That's not to say that movement doesn't help the plan, because it does.

However, if the investment vehicle doesn't move, that's not the fault of the plan, it's the fault of the investment choice. But very few investments don't have monthly movement, and that's what I used.

QUESTION 3: Are you saying that Rational Investing cannot lose money?

ANSWER: Definitely not. That would be impossible, as all investments have risk; but, here again, that's inherent in the investment vehicle, not the plan. The plan won't allow you to go broke because every adjustment is a percentage of something (portfolio value or cash), so theoretically it will always give you a viable option and action to take.

However, if, for example, you buy a company stock at $X and the next day the company files for bankruptcy, you have a gigantic loss coming, and nothing will alter that fact. Rational Investing is not perfect because the nature of investing allows for gains and losses. But if you stick with known mutual funds or corporate stocks you are on fairly safe ground. The plan makes whatever happens from that point better. It will manage your money and portfolio better than you could have done yourself.

QUESTION 4: What about using stops? In your example you didn't, yet elsewhere you recommend them.

ANSWER: Due to the percentage weighting, the plan has a form of stops built in, both in buying and selling. However, if you deem it necessary, you can stop your down-side at any point you decide. For example, in our charts you could have decided you weren't going to buy anymore if the unit price got below five dollars. You would have then ignored the buy order at four dollars. In short, you can use personally designed stop orders, but I don't recommend them.

Rational Investing is flexible, and although I don't believe any but a few should, you can adjust those features you deem necessary. I believe you'll find that those adjustments work to your disadvantage; however, it's your decision.

QUESTION 5: How much money do I have to have to start a plan for myself?

ANSWER: Everything is relative. Ten dollars to a poor man is just as important, maybe more so, than $100,000 to a rich man. That is to say, we all should invest. Invest what you can.

Hypothetically, the program works with any amount. Smaller amounts obviously limit your investment choices, but do not remove them entirely. Rational Investing, unlike so many plans, works for everyone.

QUESTION 6: Why can't I adjust along the way? For instance, if during the month the stock (assuming a stock investment choice) jumps a great deal, wouldn't it be better to make my move right then, rather than wait until the end of the month?

ANSWER: No matter what, stick to the schedule, preferably monthly. Why? Because this further takes choice away from the individual, and that's important. That's not to imply that you're not capable. Rather, it's an acknowledgement that over the long term, things average out. If you start ignoring the plan's timing on the upside, you will soon be doing so on the downside. Pretty soon you'll be on your own, refusing to believe that something so simple as the Rational Investing plan can know more than you. Like it or not, it does.

QUESTION 7:   Are you telling me to ignore my broker? What would he think of The Rational Investor?

ANSWER: What you do with your broker is your business, but I refer you to the chapter entitled "Brokers and Your Money." Full-service brokers and many investment publications realize the plan could virtually put them out of business, so I suspect they won't like it much. Discount brokers, on the other hand, won't mind since their charges aren't associated with all the fees the plan will eliminate.

Any good broker will tell you that Rational Investing does what it says it does—manages your portfolio, and produces results!

QUESTION 8:   Can I get out of my plan at some point without destroying the results?

ANSWER: Of course. You can get out at any time, but know this. If you get out at the low end you will lose money. That isn't necessary if you'll follow the plan; but, emergencies do happen, so it's possible.

On the other side, you can cash out your units if their value warrants that action. If I bought in at ten dollars, for instance, and a few months later it was twenty-two dollars, I would adjust the plan according to my feelings regarding the market. That doesn't mean I would leave the plan, but I might consider leaving my investment choice if all the signs were there. Read some of the other chapters. Certain signs will pop up along the way. For example, if I was into gold and all the signs said gold was going into a reversal, I would make an adjustment. But, and this is important, I would leave my investment choice, not the plan! Substitute bonds for gold, or whatever. Formula changes will have to be made, for instance with the entry level price, but changes can be made. So, in effect, you left the plan without actually leaving the plan.

Again, don't confuse investment choice with the plan—two different things completely. They both will affect your results, and that is why I have included general market knowledge and keys along with the plan. Put them together and they can be financial dynamite.

QUESTION 9: Do I have to set up a separate plan for each investment choice; i.e., do I have to have a mutual fund plan and a stock plan, etc.?

ANSWER: That depends on you. One plan will handle everything all at once as long as you correctly keep track of the entry level price and all the other facts and figures. For some, this may be too difficult. If that's the case, maintain two plans, three plans, or whatever is easiest for you.

Once you start using the plan you will find it very convenient, and you will not be confused no matter the number of investments. Then too, most of us have limited funds. Our figuring will be very simple, and at most we will only have one or two investment vehicles to worry about.

QUESTION 10: Why at the start of the program do you have a 50/50 split on your portfolio value and cash?

ANSWER: All things are relative and since both portfolio value and cash make the system work, we want them to start out balanced. It doesn't make any difference what the entry level price is, or where the unit price goes. You have to be able to adjust your buy/sell signals. You would negate or prejudge the market if you weighed the split any other way than even.

Granted, it may turn out that a 70/30 split would have produced more under certain conditions, but, again, over the long term, a 50/50 split will give the best results with the most protection. After the program starts taking orders, the split will be determined by the value of the unit price. Let the plan determine your starting balance for the best results.

QUESTION 11:   Why don't you have a column for commissions? You can't ignore them and be truly accurate.

ANSWER: On the contrary. Most investments have no commission, and the fact that one might think that way indicates a broker's mind set. As a rule, most investments don't happen on the stock market per se. In other chapters I mention many different vehicles.

On balance, subtracting commissions depends on your investment choice. If you follow my strong recommendation and go the mutual fund route, commissions don't have to be a reality.

Simply stated, I didn't subtract commissions because in my own plan I don't have any. If you do and wish to add another column for total accounting, it's not a bad idea. Again, Rational Investing works with stocks and it will work without them. The trouble is, most investors have come to accept the market as defined by the insiders. That makes for costly judgment or priority errors. There is another very profitable financial world out there, one that doesn't require commissions to play the game.

QUESTION 12:   Isn't it dangerous to keep buying more units as their value goes down?

ANSWER: Only if the value goes down to zero, and if you've shown some common sense in your investment vehicle that should never happen.

Actually, although the question has merit on its face, it should be obvious that most investors end up doing just the opposite. For example, when does the general public start investing in a particular stock? When its run-up becomes general knowledge. The average investor ends up buying in at or near the top end, and then watches a sizable portion of his investment disappear. The nature of the market means that most buy in at the wrong time. Reversing that trend with Rational Investing is not a mistake. The plan's weighted averaging means you buy more, as a percentage, as the price drops, which eventually limits your losses. The reverse is also true. Your sell signals will protect your profits, while letting your winners run. The percentages could be better at one extreme or the other; i.e., a more weighted factor would mean more purchases by dollar amount when the price really drops. However, that's unrealistic in most markets. We want movement, not extreme volatility, and that's what most named investments or companies offer. Our percentages are based on reality, semi-predictable movements, and safety.

QUESTION 13: With my limited funds I may have no other choice but to buy into one stock or investment. If that goes down in price and doesn't return, I will have a problem, even with Rational Investing. Is that right?

ANSWER: Yes, but that's not necessary. Elsewhere in the book, I point out the imperative of diversification. That's why I highly recommend mutual funds. They offer exactly what most readers need, and on many different fronts. You can follow the market, use the other information to spot trends, invest very little to get started, and still not have all your eggs in one basket. Also, most funds offer the investor the bonus of investing, through fractional shares, whatever dollar amount they wish (many have a fifty to one hundred dollar minimum per transaction), which makes the calculations for the plan even easier.

QUESTION 14: What about dividends? Your forms have made no provision for them.

ANSWER: This is similar to the question about commissions. There will be some dividends of course, but Rational Investing doesn't plan on them. Why? Because if you're in the market for dividends, you, generally speaking, picked the wrong reason.

For most investors dividends are a bonus. I make no provisions for them as they are not reliable in amount or frequency.

QUESTION 15: What happens if I get a bought/sold indication and it only amounts to a few dollars?

ANSWER: Obviously, that can happen. What you do about it depends on you. I ignore indications for less than one hundred dollars. That saves me work and the broker aggravation. Your investment preference should dictate the answer to this question. Use your own judgment. If the amount is small, it's not a critical issue.

QUESTION 16: The plan appears to sell out winning positions. Using your example charts you could have made more money if you were holding on and then only selling units when they reached their top of fifteen dollars. Doesn't this contradict "Winning Big, Losing Small?"

ANSWER: You and everyone else that may have come to that conclusion are making the assumption that you would be able to know when and if the top of fifteen dollars would be reached. That's the kind of seeing-into-the-future thought process that gets investors in trouble. No one knows what the future value of an investment will be. The plan understands that, so it adjusts (buys or sells) based on the present value, while still allowing for future growth. Of course, it makes allowances for reversals too.

When you start looking for tops and bottoms you get burned. Any regular stock market investor can tell you that. I repeat, no one can predict any market consistently. That's why Rational Investing works while others fail. Our plan doesn't need to interpret the market. The plan will, on occasion, take you partially out of a winning situation; however, over the long term it will always garner the most profits. The plan works. Picking the tops and bottoms of investments doesn't.

QUESTION 17: You say that Rational Investing can work with any investment vehicle, including real estate. That confuses me.

ANSWER: The only confusion in this case would be determining the unit price each month. Of course, if I was using real estate in a plan, I would make appropriate adjustments. For example, perhaps I would make my calculations every three or six months instead of monthly. Other than that, the plan is the same as with all other vehicles that one might use.

If you're using real estate, you must have substantial capital in such volume to allow for large purchases. Frankly, I would find the plan inconvenient and impractical using real estate. Obviously, people with plans that start out with a few thousand dollars can't realistically choose real estate as their investment vehicle. As mentioned earlier, to some degree your capital at any given moment will narrow your investment field. That notwithstanding, the plan's principles work with all investments. That's an important distinction that has to be made. I mention real estate to make that point.

QUESTION 18:   You have a great deal of material regarding investment vehicle choices. And yet you make a very strong case for mutual funds. If they work so well with Rational Investing, why did you waste time with the others?

ANSWER: First of all, mutual funds, as recommended throughout this book, work quite well with the plan. For most investors with smaller investment resources, mutual funds are a perfect fit, especially when first starting out.

The other information, and notice that the plan will work for other investments, is an acknowledgment that not everyone will follow my recommendation. I couldn't ignore them. Also, as your plan starts to make you rich, you may wish to leave mutual funds and go into something that requires more capital, like real estate. I wanted to give information that you could use now and in the future.

QUESTION 19:   You say in a number of places that to be in the market you have to be a pro or use one. What do you mean exactly?

ANSWER: I mean that to be in any market you must know what you're doing or you'll get hurt. That's why you need Rational Investing. In my mind, the moment you commit to the concept, you are a pro. The plan makes you one.

Carry that question further into investment vehicle
choice. If you're going to invest in investment quality
U.S. coins, you'd better be an expert in U.S. investment grade coins. If you're not, you better have a pro
you rely on (not someone you buy from!!!) for advice.
Not for advice on when and how much to buy, rather
on what to buy and at what price. The difference
should be obvious.

QUESTION 20:   Would Rational Investing have stopped
me from taking a huge loss in October of 1987 (the
Crash of '87)?

ANSWER: No, not by itself. Aberrant market corrections
and their effect cannot be factored into any plan.
However, I refer you to the case study at the end of
the book to see the positive affect of the plan in a
worst-case scenario.

Additionally, no professional has all of his or her
money in the stock market, ever. Diversification and
the plan offer as much protection as possible. You
can profit, crash or not.

QUESTION 21:   Your Weight Factor table indicates your
values, i.e., what profit is worth protecting and at
what point you should buy additional units. What if
I have different values? For instance, what if I don't
want to start turning my profits into cash until they
have appreciated a minimum of 20 percent? Can I
change the weight factors?

ANSWER: Of course, but I don't recommend it. My factors are based on cycles, not values per se, but, again,
that's a decision you have to make.

QUESTION 22:   Because the plan makes use of cycles,
doesn't it run the risk of becoming nonfunctional?
For example, if I bought a stock at five dollars and it

just keeps going up I will eventually sell out all my holdings. The reverse is also true. If the price continues to go down there will come a point at which I can do nothing.

ANSWER: That's true, but I have to ask rhetorically, when is the last time you bought a stock and it just kept going up and up? In that case you would sell out your position, but at a very great profit. Perhaps you would have made more later, but that's not what investing is all about. Your success in any market is what money you made on what money you invested. The fact is, very few investments skyrocket or completely collapse. *Profitable investing is a long-term consideration!* Don't ever forget that.

QUESTION 23: What makes Rational Investing work?

ANSWER: The plan works for one simple reason. *All markets are cyclical.* That means that only a long-term averaged investment approach will consistently win.

Since it's impossible to predict markets with any acceptable degree of accuracy, you have to stop trying. Bank on the historical fact of market cycles. That's what the plan does, and that's why it works.

13

Savings

To most people, the subject of savings is boring at best. The word immediately brings to mind the picture of a savings passbook at a local financial institution. A passbook that pays approximately 5 percent interest. A passbook that after taxes and inflation is a net loss to the depositor. It's hard to get excited about an investment vehicle like that.

I would like you to consider another definition of savings. Savings should be a systematic program, based on a percentage of your salary, that is used for the purpose of acquiring additional wealth through other investment vehicles. You can use your local bank if you choose, as location is not the criterion of a savings plan. It's not the vehicle that determines if you are saving. It's the continuum of putting aside monies on a predetermined basis that counts.

Therefore, savings can be associated with any investment vehicle. Actually, at present, using a bank or S&L for savings is the least desirable alternative. Of course, there will be times when you may wish to consider using a traditional financial institution, but, again, the vehicle is not the issue. The commitment to save is.

Savings cannot involve any form of speculation since that destroys the ability to foresee the end results of your efforts. For example, if you set aside $X per month as savings, and then speculate in commodities, how can you compute your capital in five, ten, fifteen years? Obviously you can't. It follows that even though you are setting aside monthly monies for your savings plan, you are not saving, because a savings plan has to have a reasonable expectation of planned, anticipated returns. By its very nature, speculation precludes that.

If you set aside $X per month and invest in rare coins, are you saving? Definitely. How? you may ask. Aren't rare coins speculation? No, as indicated earlier, they are not. Although I will admit you must be careful in the rare coin market, the fact is that rare investment quality coins have an acceptable and predictable track record of return. The same can be said for mutual funds, investment quality residential real estate, etc. You see, savings can take on many forms. Unfortunately, most envision the least profitable form— the savings passbook— and that causes them to reject the savings principle. That's a mistake.

Many of us, in today's financially high-pressured market, will have amassed little or nothing in the way of liquid assets. In other words, we have no savings plan. Saving money is not easy, especially now when many of us have to spend every dollar we have just to make ends meet. No, it's not easy, but it's *mandatory* for financial success. Savings are the fuel that makes Ratiional Investing work.

Many years ago, saving was something everyone did. Our grandparents were products of a financial environment that our generation cannot comprehend. They knew that if you didn't save, you would be at the mercy of an uncertain future. If you had some money in reserve, they believed you had a chance to ride through rough times.

With double-digit inflation and the arrival of the I-want-it-now generation, savings in America declined. Today we have one of the lowest savings ratios of any democratic society. Are we so smart, or are they so stupid?

The truth is, we're the stupid ones.

Savings has been replaced with things we cannot afford and in most cases don't need. Furthermore, people who save are often ridiculed by financial experts. These authorities are almost unanimous in the opinion that traditional saving is a waste of time. They want you to invest. Unfortunately, their definition of an investment is usually my definition of a speculation. That means you lose, they win.

In fairness, I cannot deny that with record inflation, coupled with normal bank savings rates, standard savings are an inferior investment. In fact, I previously drew it to your attention. But, once again, let's not confuse the vehicle used with the commitment to save. The obligation is as important today as it was in our grandparent's day. As every millionaire knows, *you must pay yourself before you pay others*. A substantial portion of your earnings must be saved each month.

For comparison, let's look at traditional financial institution savings over the last decade. Those people that used this method have retained a portion of what they earned, which is a lot more than many can say. Can the same be said for those that spent, spent, spent, on the expectation that prices were surely going to continue to rise? No, probably not, especially because most borrowers borrow for the wrong reason. They borrow for depreciating assets. The wealthy, or those that soon will be, only borrow for appreciating assets. The point here is that even though I don't recommend saving in the established sense, I believe that even those that do use traditional savings vehicles will do better than those that have no plan whatsoever. The principle of savings produces positive results, and Rational Investinvesting magnifies the benefits.

I caution you that saving requires dedication and hard work. It takes time. You can't make a million over night, but you can make a million. Saving works primarily due to the effect of accumulating numbers. That is the key to any savings plan.

In Tables 8 and 9, when I use the word savings, substitute in your mind whatever investment vehicle you want. In the examples I use a 10 percent compounded return, which is conservative. The investment vehicles you use with Rational Investing should have a much higher return expectation. Lastly, the accumulation effect can either be through interest, appreciation, inflation, or any combination. Don't get confused and think that the investments we are talking about don't pay interest. The wealthy realize that ordinarily you don't acquire riches through interest. Interest protects wealth; it seldom creates it. Appreciation, dividends, or interest all contribute to return.

These examples are used because they keep with The Rational Investor's "Golden Rule of Savings," which states: YOU MUST SAVE A MINIMUM OF 5 PERCENT OF YOUR GROSS SALARY EVERY MONTH. To further elaborate the principle of savings as a means to become financially independent, I have also included a chart for the same gross salaries, using a 10 percent savings figure for the more ambitious.

This monthly savings will go into your Rational Investing plan.

I hope you found the tables interesting. They clearly show that savings can accumulate enormously. And these

TABLE 8
5 Percent Savings
(At 10 Percent "Interest" in Dollars)

Salary	Monthly Savings	10 Years	20 Years	30 Years
20,000	83.33	17,069.73	63,278.21	188,366.46
25,000	104.17 (24.04 a week)	21,337.68	79,099.66	235,463.72
30,000	125.00 (28.85 a week)	25,605.62	94,921.11	282,560.98
35,000	145.83 (33.65 a week)	29,872.54	110,738.76	329,646.94
40,000	166.67 (38.46 a week)	34,140.49	126,560.20	376,744.21
45,000	187.50 (43.27 a week)	38,408.44	142,381.65	423,841.47
50,000	208.33 (48.07 a week)	42,675.35	158,199.30	470,927.43

charts only reflect a return of 10 percent. Even in a weak market you should be able to surpass that rate.

To make the point, look at the 10 percent savings chart in the salary line of $30,000.00. After ten years you have a balance of $51,211.24. During that time you deposited a total of $30,000.00, which means your "interest" is $21,211.24. At the twenty year mark, you have a balance of $189,842.21. During that time you actually paid in a total of $60,000.00, which means you have earned interest of a whopping $129,842.21. You have accumulated

TABLE 9
10 Percent Savings
(At 10 Percent "Interest" in Dollars)

Salary	Monthly Savings	10 Years	20 Years	30 Years
20,000	166.66	34,139.46	126,566.41	376,732.90
25,000	208.33 (48.07 a week)	42,675.35	158,199.31	470,927.40
30,000	250.00 (57.69 a week)	51,211.24	189,842.21	565,121.90
35,000	291.66 (67.30 a week)	59,745.08	221,477.51	659,293.80
40,000	333.33 (76.92 a week)	68,280.97	253,120.41	753,488.40
45,000	375.00 (86.53 a week)	76,816.87	284,763.31	847,682.90
50,000	416.66 (96.15 a week)	85,350.71	316,398.61	941,854.80

interest equal to more than double what you paid in. The figures become staggering the further down the line we go.

And all we require is 5 to 10 percent of your gross income. Even if you are forty-five years old when you start, you can amass a sizable fortune by sixty-five. The savings principle works regardless of age. And if you don't save, I can assure you that you will be substantially poorer in twenty years than those that did.

There's another characteristic to this methodical approach that is often overlooked: Percentage savings is inflation proof in an indirect way. Almost everyone in times of high inflation receives a cost-of-living wage increase along with their yearly raise. Since your savings plan is predicated on a percentage, your savings positioning should remain at a movable constant that reflects the status quo. In the charts, I used a specific yearly amount to show how investments grow monthly. In actuality, your balance in ten or twenty years should be far in excess of the charts. Again, the percentage factor. You may start out with a salary of twenty thousand dollars per year, but wind up at seventy-five thousand dollars at career end. Obviously then, your monthly savings amount will constantly increase and, consequently, so will your ultimate balance.

Clearly, I have not taken into account all the possibilities of savings as they apply to your individual plan. It is up to you to tailor the specifics. Here's one interesting alternative: Although many families have two breadwinners today, not all need both to meet expenses. That means that large numbers can be plugged into the savings principle. To make the point, look at Table 10.

This table assumes a total second salary is being deposited monthly. This has several advantages. Unlike an IRA, you can put in as much as you wish, and withdraw when you want without penalty. It has tangible, long-term benefits that can, when necessary, be used immediately.

If your spouse were able to work for just ten years, and were making a salary of $12,000.00, you would have a balance of $204,844.98 at the end of that term. Not bad, you earned $12,000.00 for ten years and in return you could receive a guaranteed income of $24,581.40 (at 12 percent per year - $2,048.45 per month) for life and never touch the $204,844.98 principal. Of course, saving the entire second income is not always possible, but even saving a portion results in substantial accumulation.

Remember, these are conservative estimates in every case. Rational Investing will do far better. Percentage

TABLE 10
Second Income Invested
(At 10 Percent "Interest" in Dollars)

Salary (Monthly)	10 Years	20 Years	30 Years
500.00 (6,000.00 a year)	102,422.49	379,684.41	1,130,243.80
1,000.00 (12,000 a year)	204,844.98	759,368.82	2,260,487.90
1,500.00 (18,000.00 a year)	307,267.46	1,139,053.20	3,390,731.80

savings and dedication on your part will allow the system to perform at its maximum. *Savings plus investment management equals profits.* The plan provides the management. It's up to you to provide the savings.

14

What About Your Cash?

Liquidity is very important to the Rational Investor. It allows you, due to its judicious balance of investments and cash, to make immediate changes as circumstances dictate. But your cash should provide more than instant liquidity. Cash management should add to the total portfolio return in the form of interest.

As should be apparent, I believe in reasonable safety for the investor. Those who disdain safety are speculators, and, to repeat, this book isn't for them. You might think that I would recommend that you put all your cash deposits in a federally insured bank or savings and loan association. Right? Wrong!

Federal deposit insurance is a myth in many ways. The FSLIC has collapsed. Their insurance program as it related to the consumer, failed. In effect, they declared bankruptcy, and we are stuck with the bill, proving conclusively that government-backed insurance means consumers are insuring themselves.

The FDIC is almost as bad. They have fractional reserves for the deposits they insure. These small reserve-to-deposit ratios were acceptable until the banking industry started to set post-Depression records for the number of bank closings. Previously, we averaged 12 bank closings per year. In 1990, there were 169 (that's one every 1.54 business days). The FDIC used to have, on average, less than 100 banks on their trouble list (the list of banks one step away from being closed). They now have almost 1,000 banks on that list. Under these circumstances, their reserves are highly suspect and quite possibly will, at some point, suffer the same fate as those of the FSLIC. Preventive actions may be taken, but, based on the history of government banking agencies, I doubt it.

It's a stock bit of reassuring rhetoric that the FDIC is backed by "the full faith and credit of the federal government." That's true of course, but I direct your attention to the fact that the federal government is over three trillion in debt (if you include government guarantees the debt escalates to almost TWELVE TRILLION dollars!). Where does this put your "full faith and credit of the federal government?" It means that FDIC insurance, which is traveling the same road as the now defunct FSLIC, is backed by a government that is verifiably bankrupt. The fact is, there is no security here, unless you count the government's ability to print fiat money. But who wants to get paid back with a dollar that is worth perhaps pennies in buying power?

This subject is important for two reasons: first, you must understand that many financial markets are not stable or backed by anything other than trust. Destroy the trust in the system and you have created conditions ripe for disaster. That's one reason why the Crash of '87 happened so rapidly on Black Monday. It didn't start because trust was destroyed, but once the market started to rapidly retreat, panic ensued because people had lost faith. The balloon had been punctured. The same principle holds true with financial institutions. Clearly then, the safety of your local bank, regardless of its apparent stability, is highly suspect. Worse yet, your bank could have an unprofessional management team. The FDIC says substantial numbers of financial institution closings are prompted by mismanagement or illegal insider actions by bank directors or officers.

Secondly, this insurance feature of banking institutions is used against the customer. This is especially true when banks court the affluent elderly who remember the Great Depression and therefore fear the loss of savings more than adults of working age. Elderly investors, and others, forgo better interest rate returns for the perceived safety of the FDIC insurance. *Traditional financial institutions pay less interest than the market will bear.* You lose potential income when you deposit with them. The difference between bank interest rates and other financial options can be anywhere from 1 to 3 percentage points, or in some cases, more.

Not concerned about that seemingly small amount? Rational Investing is going to allow you to have cash, a lot of it, and 1 to 3 percentage points will cost you a great deal. On one hundred thousand dollars you could be giving up three thousand dollars a year, thirty thousand dollars for ten years, more with compounding. A few percentage points are worth fighting for. Most financial institutions thrive on that differential. They know that a small margin applied to the right volume brings huge profits. That's something you should know too.

Consider something else that banks don't advertise: Presently, FDIC insurance only covers up to one hundred thousand dollars. And that may be lowered in the near future. Congress has indicated such intentions. Above that, you're out of luck if something goes wrong at the bank. By switching account names, etc., you can increase that coverage, but not by enough. Regardless, the single account coverage is still only one hundred thousand dollars, and your plan is going to exceed that by a large amount.

To show you how the insurance really works, and how the banks use it to their advantage, let's look at a bank IRA. Whenever they advertise for regular savings and checking deposits, banks let the customer know that they have FDIC insurance and the market doesn't. They focus your attention on the safety factor and make money in the process. But what happens when they advertise for IRA's? They show you charts and graphs that tell you you'll be a millionaire at retirement if you deposit with them. It all sounds great. Nowhere in the ad will you see a note indicating that perhaps nine-tenths of that million will not be insured. They promote the insurance when it's profitable to their deposit base, and ignore it completely when they are advertising for deposits that at some point won't be insured.

Strip away all the tinsel, and the insurance issue is a fraud. The corporate assets of most reputable investment firms are a far better insurance policy than what the financial institutions offer. And that brings us to the alternative to traditional cash savings vehicles: money markets.

Money funds as offered on the market historically pay more, in some cases a lot more, than traditional financial institutions. In the not-too-distant past their rates were almost double that of banks. But even if that rate differential never returns, it still, in most instances, pays to ignore banks. Money market accounts offer numerous possible benefits, such as the ability to write checks at no cost, immediate flexibility, day-of-deposit-to-day-of-withdrawal/compounded and paid daily interest, statement accounting, convenience for your Rational Investing plan, etc. Every money market or fund account has its own features so you will have to shop around. Take the time, it's worth it.

In an earlier chapter I reviewed mutual funds. That chapter includes a list of funds you may wish to investigate. When you do, ask about their money market accounts. Having both funds with the same corporation is quite convenient, and makes your plan even easier to manage. It allows you to switch markets using the indicator of The Twelve Percent Investment Rule. For those of you who don't like having all your money with one firm, you can have several funds within your plan, all with different firms. It's similar to buying numerous different stocks in the same field. It really doesn't matter if you have one money market account or five. Do what's right for you.

Every money market fund has slightly different conditions, so I urge caution. Understand what you are buying. Stick with corporations you know by name. That same advice is true for all your investments. Investigate. Know the firms you are doing business with.

I believe most people don't use their liquid funds correctly. They may agonize over their other investments (stocks, bonds, etc.) and then let thousands of dollars sit in the bank earning virtually nothing. A gap of this kind in a financial plan can be very costly.

Cash is an asset. Treat it like one.

PART IV

15

Brokers and Your Money

The number of stockbrokers who have been charged with
or found guilty of Security Exchange Commission violations is frighteningly large. Questionable tactics, such as
churning, selling marginal securities, and high-pressure
selling techniques, as well as flagrant criminal violations,
are giving the extremely profitable brokerage houses
cause for concern because the public is starting to ask
embarrassing questions.

I believe the reason for brokerage abuse is simple. The
commission sales system, which pays brokers for what
they sell rather than for what they earn for their clients,
is the root of the evil.

Full commission brokers justify their fees by indicating
that the customer is paying not only for the transaction
itself, but also for expert advice. The support system for
that advice is expensive, and, when used, that cost should
be borne by the customer. However, the vast majority of
trade decisions are made solely by the consumer, and the
broker becomes nothing more than a middleman. In short,

millions of customers every day are charged for expert advice when none was asked for or given. Unfortunately, although brokerage houses may have large support expenses, they bill for individual transactions.

In general, individual brokers are paid approximately 40 percent of the fees they generate. The house may have a sliding scale for their direct consumer charges, depending on the volume of sales. Does this fee schedule make for excessive charges? The average broker in 1986 made eighty thousand dollars. Based on what he produced for you, is your broker worth that much? I doubt it.

Of course, the payment system is only part of the problem. There are other aspects of trading that are objectionable. For instance, your broker may be withholding information that would allow you to make an intelligent financial decision. Unknown to many investors, sponsors of certain investments offer incentives to the broker or the house for selling their product. The brokers end up encouraging you and others to invest in vehicle X, or tax shelter Y, etc., without ever caring if it truly fits your wants and needs. All they are thinking about is the free trip to the Bahamas they're going to earn if they can sign up enough people. I believe that all brokers, investment councelors, bankers, etc., should be forced by law to reveal any and all possible conflicts of interest whenever they are selling an investment to the general public. But until they are, you should be on guard.

This full-disclosure position is one that the S.E.C. should embrace immediately to restore some integrity to the investment industry. Their actions to date have been suspiciously slow.

The brokerage investment industry is highly regulated, yet broker abuses continue to escalate. Why? Although the regulations are more than adequate, they are seldom enforced. Couple this with the fact that brokers are constantly pressured by their house to sell, sell, sell, and you have a blueprint for consumer disaster. Simply stated, brokers who don't meet their quotas are soon without employment. It is easy to see why many forget that they are first legally and morally charged with the financial well-being of their clients. The reality of the industry is that sales come first.

Industry changes are called for. Specifically:

1. Full-service brokers should be remunerated on a straight salary basis, thus removing the incentive to churn accounts.

2. Full-service brokers should charge only for those services that are performed. A charge for each aspect of a transaction should be clearly presented, e.g., a transaction bill, a research bill, a support bill. Bulk billing hides the customer's true cost and makes shopping for brokers almost impossible.

3. Stop the policy of hidden sales incentives.

4. Mandate full disclosure of all conflicting positions.

These specifics are germane to the financial industry as a whole, not just to stock brokerage. Any individual or corporation that deals with others' monies should be obligated to be responsible to the fiduciary relationship. But until that's true you should take the following steps to ensure your safety:

1. Whenever possible, take delivery of your investments.

2. Use a discount house. They can save you as much as 70 percent of your trading costs. In fact, if you need the advice of a full-service broker, you probably shouldn't be in the market. With Rational Investing you have no need for a full-service relationship.

3. Cultivate brokerage house contacts and let them spend time and effort feeding you information and

free advice while trying to entice your account, which they will never get.

4. If you have a problem with a specific broker, contact the house's main office with a formal written complaint. These days, with consumer awareness heightened (along with S.E.C. investigations), most houses will respond and try to resolve the matter. Remember, most brokers and the houses they represent are reputable. It's the system and certain individuals who abuse it that cause problems.

5. If, after trying to correct a situation, you are unsuccessful, contact the Securities and Exchange Commission, 450 Fifth St., Washington, DC 20001–2719. Phone: (202) 272–2650. They will assign your complaint to one of their regional offices.

To be complete on this subject, we have to review the distasteful possibility that you may run into a dishonest or incompetent broker. Did you ever get the feeling you are the most unlucky investor in the world? Does every hot stock you invest in get cold three seconds after your buy order is completed? Are most, if not all, your trades losers and the winners don't come close to compensating for them? Has your broker ever used buzzwords like, "...going to double in price", "Can't miss", "Have to get in now", "We'll both be rich", "A once in a lifetime opportunity"? If you recognize any or all of the above, your broker may be injuring you, or at least isn't your best choice for a financial adviser. Most investors make a mistake with their broker and allow him to become the dominant player in the relationship. You should never forget that he works for you. Because of that, you should demand results. If he doesn't produce, fire him. It's sadly ironic that we see so many aggressive business types who will not hesitate to fire an employee for one small mistake, and yet will allow their broker to make ten, twenty, thirty thousand dollars worth of bad judgements and never say a word.

With totally dishonest brokers you have additional problems. They not only cost you funds with bad advice, but even when they are right their dishonesty can penalize you. As previously noted, one of the best ways to avoid broker and stock illegalities is to take delivery of your investments. Your broker can't use them if he doesn't have them. Some readers may ask why this is so important. Street-named stock allows the broker to sell the stock and use the proceeds, pledge the stock for personal borrowing, or leverage your stock for his or her transactions.

It should be pointed out that some brokers will tell you that abuse of street-named stock isn't a problem since Securities Investor Protection Corporation (SIPC) insurance protects the investor's securities. That protection is often misunderstood. It protects against loss or theft, not price valuation. Therefore, if your broker is dishonest, he can use your stock for months on end, even though you may have wished to sell. When the certificates are finally located and processed as they should have been originally, they may have only a fraction of their previous value. Loss of value is not insured. To protect against this kind of loss, have the stock in your name and take delivery of the certificates, or have the stocks registered in your name and ensure that you receive a copy of the registration.

If your broker is constantly giving you excuses, and time keeps passing without your stock showing up, write the SEC. I would also suggest a letter to the National Association of Securities Dealers, Inc., 1735 K. Street NW, Washington, D.C. 20006. Phone: (202) 728-8000.

Why all of this discussion of broker abuse in a book that outlines an investment program? What does this have to do with anything? Nothing, and everything. It has absolutely no effect on what Rational Investing will produce for its users. It has everything to do with what happens to your net profit after the fact. The plan is going to make you richer than you may have ever thought possible. I don't want you to lose it.

Whether you like it or not, you are probably going to have to deal with a broker of some sort. That means you are vulnerable. A mistake in the placing of your trust can mean the loss of every penny our plan makes. An incompetent counselor can cost you a small fortune. A dishonest broker or adviser can take it all.

Recent developments indicate that stockbrokers are, contrary to what they would have you believe, unregulated potential adversaries. Since the entire securities industry is based in some part on trust, one dishonest broker is too many. This has become an even more important issue since the Supreme Court and the Securities Exchange Commission made it easier for the dishonest broker or brokerage house to defraud their clients. In the decision of Shearson/American Express vs. McMahon, the court, in effect, took away the right of the investor to sue for fraud Further, it doesn't matter how large the loss or the flagrance of the violation. The only investor option is arbitration supervised by the securities industry itself. If that doesn't sound fair to you, that's because it's not. Whenever you allow an industry to police itself, you put the consumer at risk. The SEC, for the purpose of their convenience and public appearance, has dissociated itself from the process. More than likely they will assign your complaint to a stock exchange for review and conclusion. Arbitration on these grounds allows for virtually no discovery, no depositions, no consumer legal representations, nor any other aspect of a fraud investigation that one might expect.

In the end, it's your word against the broker or house, and the winner will be decided by fellow industry brothers. Even if you do win, the decision will have no affect on future cases of the same kind, or even those involving the same broker or house. Why? Because, since criminal charges have nothing to do with arbitration, the brokers can be assured that they are insulated from true justice. If the brokers lose, they are only required to make restitution to the claimant. If they perpetrated the same fraud on others, unless other victims filed an action of their own, no class action benefits accrue. Please understand how serious this is. Brokers are not discouraged from continued fraud.

Just in case you may feel that I am being an alarmist and confrontational for no reason, pull out the account forms from your brokerage house. Read them cover to cover, and see if you can't find the section that waives your right to sue for fraud. Nearly all the new account forms from major houses have this waiver. You agreed, assuming you read it when you signed on, or understood it if you read it, that no matter what happens you will not sue the house or their representative for fraud. Strip away the jargon and it means that if you want to play their game, you have to play by their rules. The Supreme Court and the SEC just made that the law of the land. The dishonest broker has just had his or her license to steal validated.

Of course, any reasonable investor knew all along that the market had some major equity flaws, but this is too much. If you took your car to a garage that made you sign a waiver that stated no matter how bad the repairs, no matter how unprofessional their service, no matter if their errors caused an accident to your family five minutes after you drove away, no matter what, you wouldn't sue, would you allow them to work on your car? Most assuredly not! Yet, investors are asked to give a like all-inclusive waiver to their broker. Remember, we're not talking about bad advice here; we're talking about criminal fraud.

What can you do? Now more than ever, understand that your broker is a potential antagonist. Any industry that wants consumers to waive their right to sue for fraud must feel there is a very good chance one might have just cause for a suit. Start watching your monthly reports. Check your mutual fund statements. Ask where your stock is. Review your money market statement. Take nothing for granted. Your financial future may depend on you being responsible and aggressive. If you do decide to use arbitration, and in some cases this may be wise or unavoidable, understand what you're up against. Unless you understand the unfairness of the rules, you stand little chance of being successful with your claim.

Rational Investing will produce financial success. It can't, however, stop you from being cheated. It can't stop you from using bad advice. It can't stop you from being robbed. Only your vigilance can prevent that.

16

Stopping a Scam

In the last chapter I spoke of the need for cautious fore-thought when dealing with your broker. This goes double when buying financial products from anyone you don't know. Too often there's an element of deception, if not outright fraud, involved. Financial investment scams are a billion-dollar-a-year business, and the average customer loss of five thousand dollars is never recovered.

Their victims include doctors, lawyers, and other groups that one wouldn't expect to be fooled. But the key to a scam's success is the victim's greed, and social or professional position does not protect anyone from that very human frailty.

Regardless of why a fraud occurs, you should know that your first and most powerful line of defense against financial con artists is a series of questions that will expose the scam for exactly what it is. Good con artists know that they cannot afford to answer questions that call for verifiable answers, which means the very act of not answering your inquiries is cause enough for your refusing to become involved. Knowing that they, as a defense, try to prevent you from asking questions by taking the lead and asking you questions that call for a planned response. For instance, "Certainly you'd be interested in hearing about a fantastic investment opportunity. One that has a guaranteed return of a minimum 35 percent, and with absolutely no risk." They have a whole series of these questions, all designed to hook the victim, and, more important, stop him or her from asking questions.

Understand this: Investment scams are run by people that are extremely good at what they do. They have a contingent reaction for every move you make. They are dedicated and hardworking. They make hundreds of contacts a day, so don't think you will realize you are talking to a swindler. Thousands of victims thought the same thing.

These are the questions to ask:

1. WILL YOU SEND ME YOUR ENTIRE PROPOSAL THROUGH THE MAIL? A con artist won't want to do this because written evidence is something that can be used in court. These people, if ever caught, want it to be your word against theirs. Further, mailings take time, and that's something that works against them. It gives you too much time to think.

2. WHERE DID YOU GET MY NAME AND PHONE NUMBER? If you hear a response that says you are on their select list or you were recommended, watch out. Some scams purchase names from other scams. Others just use the phone book. Still others buy legitimate phone lists from reputable financial firms.

3. WOULD YOU BE WILLING TO EXPLAIN YOUR PROPOSAL TO MY ATTORNEY (accountant or financial adviser)? Obviously, they don't want you to receive the benefit of another opinion, especially from an

expert, so you will usually get a response like, "I'd really like to, but there just isn't time. By the time we could get together, this opportunity will be history."

4. WHAT ARE THE REAL RISKS INVOLVED? For all intents and purposes, there are no risk-free investments. It follows then that if you're told there is no risk, you are talking to a liar or fool. If he does admit to a small risk, ask for a percentage factor. Once he's committed to one, ask for substantiation of that figure. At this point a con artist will probably hang up or leave your office since he will know you are too much trouble.

5. WHAT FEDERAL AGENCY IS YOUR FIRM REGULATED BY? If he or she gives you a name, explain that you will be making an inquiry prior to considering an investment.

6. (For a phone solicitation) WHEN AND WHERE CAN WE MEET TO DISCUSS THIS MATTER? (Assuming that you're interested.) Con artists will seldom allow this since, if you demand to see them at their office, you would find out they work in a boiler room. Other contacts are too time-consuming, so they'll probably pass.

7. WHAT BANK DOES YOUR FIRM DO BUSINESS WITH? Tell him you are going to survey the bank to establish how long they have had an account, etc. A good bank won't give an individual that information on a routine basis, but a con artist won't be able to take that chance. He'll probably hang up.

8. WILL YOU SEND ME YOUR PROSPECTUS? If they don't have one, or "There just isn't time", be wary.

9. CAN I HAVE A LISTING OF BUSINESS REFERENCES? Only accept banks, other name-recognizable

investment firms, etc. Don't rely on names of individuals. Con artists have people that front as their references. You want verifiable companies.

10. WHAT TRADE ORGANIZATIONS ARE YOU A MEMBER OF? If he or she doesn't have any trade references, stay away. If he or she gives you some, check them out.

Investment scams are as varied as the intelligence and imagination of their perpetrators. Don't think you've "heard 'em all", because you haven't.

And, don't think a fraud can't happen to you, because it can. Human nature says that if the right con comes along at the right time, you are at risk. But, you can protect yourself by asking questions and verifying answers.

Some scams work over the phone; others work in person. Some go for the whole nine yards immediately; others hook you and then build on the deception. No one can give you an outline of all the scams since there are new ones being thought up while you're reading this. However— and this is critical— you can stop them all. Ask our ten questions, follow up, and you will be assured, as much as humanly possible, that you're on solid ground.

It helps to remember that almost all scams depend on greed to make the whole plan work. The old saying can't be denied: "If it sounds too good to be true, it probably is."

Lastly, if you miss the signs of a scam at its start, remember this: Most scams use pressure in terms of time. If the sales representative keeps telling you about the urgency of the opportunity, watch out. ANY INVESTMENT THAT HAS TO BE MADE IMMEDIATELY SHOULD NOT BE MADE AT ALL! When it comes to protecting your finances, you can never err on the side of caution.

Here are a few agencies that can offer assistance if you do get involved in a financial fraud:

1. FEDERAL TRADE COMMISSION
    Office of Investment Fraud
    Washington, D.C. 20580
    202-523-3598

2. SECURITIES EXCHANGE COMMISSION
    450 Fifth St., N.W.
    Washington, D.C. 20549
    202-272-2650

3. STATES ATTORNEY'S OFFICE
    (check your local phone book)

Additional agencies are listed in the Assistance Directory chapter. These offices can offer help, but, in complete candor, very seldom do they get the victim's money back.

Let's get to the real bottom line. Remember, if you are contacted by a financial firm or person you believe to be reputable, ask our questions, and verify the answers. If you get a phone call or a visit from someone not personally known to you who tries to sell you financial products, terminate the conversation immediately. It's really that simple.

You can't afford to lose your Rational Investing profits to a scam.

17

Greed Is Expensive

Financial markets are fueled by greed. There's nothing fundamentally wrong with that.

We all want to make more money for a variety of sound reasons, from saving for retirement to supplementing our present income. That's to be applauded. However, being one of the players in the system is not the problem. The problem arises when greed starts eclipsing your financial logic. That's when things go wrong.

Every con artist works their scam based on some form of excessive greed on the part of the victim. No elaboration is necessary since we discussed this in depth in the last chapter. However, greed doesn't always have to be applied to a rip-off to cause difficulty. A more subtle greed in legitimate markets is also to be avoided.

Remember this simple but valuable lesson: HIGHER RETURNS ALWAYS MEAN HIGHER RISK.

You see, even in legitimate markets your greed can cause you to lose perspective. It can cause those that are looking for investments to end up with a speculation. In that case you become your own con artist by deceiving yourself. True, your broker may help you down the road, but for the most part you're responsible.

Knowing your needs and expectations is necessary for financial success. Once that is determined you shouldn't vary from your plan. Don't let greed talk you into commodity futures when you really belong in blue chip stocks. A misplaced priority judgment like that will produce results that are disappointing at best, disastrous at worst.

Of course, the greed factor in legitimate markets also causes investors to look for exact tops and bottoms. It causes them to hold on when they should sell and sell when they should hold on. Regardless of the actual circumstances, greed in the market can compel many to make many erroneous judgments that, if they had it to do over again, they would do differently.

Believe it or not, greed becomes a factor even with those who opt for perhaps the most conservative investment, a traditional savings plan.

Generally speaking, interest rates for most savings plans have limited progressive scope; for example, the six month time certificate of deposit (TCD) may be at 7 percent, the one year TCD at 7.5 percent, the two and one half year TCD at 8.25 percent, and so on. Unfortunately, those savers that have a choice will more than likely take the higher rate. Let's compare the six month and the two and one half year certificates. There is only a 1.25 percentage point difference between the two. The question then becomes, is losing two years liquidity worth the dollar differential the 1.25 percentage points represent? Almost always the answer is a resounding NO. This is especially true when interest rates are low. In that case your downside is minimal; i.e., rates can only go so low. The upside, however, could be substantial. If your money is locked in, you will lose the interest differential between what your money is earning and what it could have been earning had you stayed liquid. Also, if you need that money during the term of the TCD agreement, you either have to borrow against the certificate, at a much higher interest rate, or withdraw funds at a substantial penalty. The point being: *never let rates alone dictate your investment choices!*

I have given you three basic examples of how the greed factor can cost you money when allowed to control your judgment from the most flagrant, a scam, to the most conservative, traditional savings.

Certainly there are exceptions, when greed and providence caused an unusual windfall for some lucky person, but investing isn't supposed to be a crap shoot. Frankly, when I do hear of such cases, the party involved, because of their avaricious nature, eventually gives back their winnings; so it might be said that greed ultimately won. For the rest of us it is prudent to remember that greed is a player in all financial markets. There is nothing wrong with that as long as you recognize the destructive nature of greed's compelling force. I mention it here for perspective. Keep in mind, the Rational Investor sees investing as a long-term opportunity. If short-term greed causes you to deviate from the plan, I can guarantee you'll find that you made an expensive mistake.

18

Conclusion

Rational Investing is potentially the most powerful investment plan ever conceived.

It eliminates human error and investment frailties. It protects your investment, while maximizing its results. It protects your profits. It gives you stop-loss orders within the system. In short, if you follow the plan you will be rewarded beyond what most could produce in even the best possible market conditions. And you do so without being a market genius. As you've seen, the plan doesn't need solid gold investments to make it work. You can make money even if the investment vehicle doesn't. That may be the most important feature of the plan.

Much of the additional nonplan information in the book is to help you choose the vehicles you will invest in. As mentioned time and time again, the plan doesn't do that by itself. The plan is an account maintenance technique. But, armed with all the guidelines outlined, your choice and decisions should be very easy to determine. Rational

Investing is flexible in your choice of options, but not in its design; i.e., if you choose X to invest in, and then change your mind a week later, that's fine, but don't expect the plan to work to its maximum under those circumstances. The plan takes time to produce. It doesn't take decades like savings plans, but it takes time nevertheless. Consequently, any time you feel like changing horses in the middle of the stream, you can because the vehicle, within reason, is not that important. Long-term planning is. If your investment choice is remotely viable, the plan will work. Again, the vehicle doesn't have to go through the roof to make things happen. The plan makes adjustments along the way. That's why various percentages have been weighted. Frankly, assuming a reasonable investment choice, the only time you have to make changes is when we shift from market to money market. Technically, that's not a vehicle change. It's an option call based on the economy.

To reiterate, within reason the plan doesn't depend on investment knowledge. Of course, if you invest in some fly-by-night vehicle (probably offered by a cold phone solicitation or your unproductive broker), you're on your own. On the other hand, if you stick with names and companies you know, the plan will produce, and produce, and produce. The variables, as outlined in various chapters, will make the plan work even better. If you see the swing when interest rates and inflation start going up together, or vice versa, you may wish to invest in another mutual fund, etc. It's not necessary, but if the move is timed right, all the better. The vehicle can be changed, if necessary and dictated by facts, but the plan can't. If it says sell, you'd better sell. If it says buy, buy. The moment you ignore the keys you ruin the results. Over the long run, even though you might be right occasionally, the plan will produce more than intuition can.

Rational Investing is necessary for two basic reasons: first, financial markets are weighed against nonprofessionals; second, even if they weren't, nonprofessionals would make too many mistakes on their own.

Add that up and you have unquestioned results, all negative. The investors lose money or make less than they should have. Rational Investing ensures that within the parameters of realistic expectations, that doesn't happen.

The most important thing the plan does is offer mathematical, totally objective account management. Over time, and with very little money with which to start, it can make you a millionaire. This isn't one of those plans that offers wealth, as long as you have the substantial capital to get started. You can start out with practically nothing and add to it along the way. This plan has no bounds, it requires no market expert to help you, and it doesn't depend on the market for results. Like this book, the plan has many aspects that overlap and dovetail. Although it may appear redundant, it's not. It's an investment gestalt that should bring you to the undeniable realization that the plan works.

Don't let its simplicity fool you. It will only take a few minutes a month to produce extraordinary profit. You and the plan can do in seconds what most investors can't do in hours, days, months or years. I believe you will look back one day and realize that your decision to utilize Rational Investing was the best investment decision you ever made.

YOUR INVESTMENT POTENTIAL HAS NEVER HELD SUCH PROMISE!

APPENDICES

Glossary

Investmentese causes confusion for many investors. I hope this glossary will assist you in understanding your choices and opportunities.

ANNUITY: A contract, usually with an insurance company, that pays a fixed amount of money at given times over a specified term.

ARBITRAGE: The simultaneous sale of an asset purchased. The arbitrager's profit margin is the difference between the buy and the sell price. In effect, there is no sale, and the arbitrager simply acts as a middleman.

ASKING PRICE: The price at which a seller of an asset offers to sell.

ASSET: Anything of value.

BAG: A unit of trade for investment coins. A bag comprises coins of any denomination the face value of which totals one thousand dollars.

BALANCE OF PAYMENTS: The total monetary value of any country's financial dealings with the rest of the world.

BALANCE SHEET: A corporate statement showing a company's assets, liabilities, and capital.

BANK HOLIDAY: A period of time when banks are closed to the public. They are not legally obligated to accept deposits or allow withdrawals during this time. The most famous bank holiday was during the Depression.

BANKRUPTCY: A condition where one cannot pay one's debts, and liabilities exceed assets. There are various legal forms of bankruptcy.

BEAR MARKET: A period of time when the price trend of stocks or other investment vehicles is in a strong pattern of downward movement.

BEARER INSTRUMENT: Any negotiable instrument— stock, bond, check, etc.— that isn't made payable to a specifically named person or entity. Whoever has it in his or her possession is considered the owner.

BEARISH: Believing that a bear market is coming or is here.

BID PRICE: The price a buyer is willing to pay for a purchase.

BOOK VALUE: The value of a company's stock. The figure is arrived at by taking company equity and dividing it by the total number of outstanding shares.

BROKER: A middleman for the stock market.

BULL MARKET: A period of time when the price trend of stocks, bonds, etc., is in a strong pattern of upward movement.

BULLION: Precious metals, usually in bar form.

BULLION COIN: An investment coin sold for the value of its precious metal content rather than its scarcity.

BULLISH: Believing a bull market is coming or is here.

CALL OPTION: The right to purchase a set quantity of stock or commodities at a given price if done so before a certain agreed upon date.

CAPITAL: The net assets of any corporation or person.

CAPITAL GAIN: A profit made from the sale of an investment.

CARRYING CHARGES: The storing or interest charge on an investment.

CASH: A medium of exchange.

CERTIFICATE OF DEPOSIT: A deposit of money for a specified period of time at a specified rate of interest. The certificate itself is a negotiable instrument.

CLOSED END INVESTMENT COMPANY: A company that invests its shareholders' monies in other companies, usually through the purchase of shares.

COLLATERAL: An asset used to secure a loan. In the case of a default, the lender has the right to sell the asset to pay the debt.

CONTENT: The amount of precious metal in a bullion coin.

CONVERTIBLE CURRENCY: A currency that can be exchanged for an established commodity, usually a precious metal. The U.S., of course, uses fiat money, which is not convertible.

CONVERTIBLE SECURITY: A security that can be exchanged for another known security or commodity at the order of the owner.

CREDIT: As a liability, obtaining borrowed money. As an asset, a deposit to your account.

CURRENCY: Government-issued money.

CUSTODIAL ACCOUNT: Any account where one holds the assets of another.

CYCLE: As used in market terms, the recurring pattern of events.

DEALER: Like a broker, someone who buys and sells for others. But, unlike a broker, the dealer also buys and sells for his or her own account.

DEBIT: Any form of withdrawal from your accounts.

DEFLATION: A decrease in general prices usually caused by a reduction in the money supply.

DEMAND DEPOSIT: Your checking account.

DEPOSIT ACCOUNT: Any account that is paid interest.

DEPRESSION: An economic upheaval where the standard of living is greatly reduced for the general population.

DEVALUATION: Lowering the redemption value of an asset. In general terms this is normally done by governments with their currency.

DISCOUNT: The amount that an asset is sold for below its value or sale price.

DISCOUNT RATE: The interest rate the Federal Reserve charges member commercial banks for the privilege of borrowing money.

DISINFLATION: A time span when the inflation rate is declining.

DOWNSIDE RISK: The possible monetary decline risk of an asset decreasing in value.

EARNED INCOME: Your salary, wages, etc.

ECONOMICS: The study of how people and countries use resources.

EQUITY: The net value of an asset; i.e., its value minus its liabilities.

EXCHANGE CONTROL: Regulations restricting the export or import of certain currencies.

EXCHANGE RATE: The value of one currency expressed in the value of another currency.

FACE VALUE: The value promised to a bondholder when the bond has matured.

FIAT MONEY: Money not convertible to a commodity. Its value derives from an intangible belief by the market.

FIDUCIARY: One that holds the assets of another for the purposes of investment. For example, your bank accounts.

FLUCTUATION: The changing worth, up or down, of an asset.

FORWARD CONTRACT: A contract agreement to deliver goods at a future date for a specific price agreed upon when the contract was drawn.

FORWARD PRICE: The price of goods contained in a forward contract.

FREE MARKET: A market unencumbered by government. In real terms, no such modern market exists.

FUTURES CONTRACT: A forward contract for buying and selling commodities (gold, wheat, cattle, copper, etc.).

HEDGE: A side investment purchased to offset conceivable losses in another investment.

INFLATION: Too much money chasing too few goods. Caused by government, not the private sector.

INTEREST RATE DIFFERENTIAL: The difference between two rates of interest. Example: A bank pays 5.5 percent interest on savings while charging 13 percent for loaning the same monies to others.

INVESTMENT COMPANY: A company that invests its shareholders' monies in investments, normally the stock market, of the company's choosing.

INVESTMENT VEHICLE: Any form of investment. For example: mutual funds, time certificates of deposit, real estate, investment coins, stocks, bonds.

LEGAL TENDER: A form of money designated acceptable by the government as payment for all legal debts.

LEVERAGED TRANSACTION: Involve a high degree of speculation. Basically, a trade made on equity or a portion thereof.

LIABILITY: A financial obligation.

LIMIT ORDER: Offering to buy if the price falls below a certain price or to sell if it rises above a certain price.

LIQUIDATION: The sale of assets.

LIQUIDITY: The ability to turn an asset into immediate cash. Real estate is not liquid. Mutual funds are.

MARGIN: The amount of equity an investor has as expressed in a percentage of the value of a margin account or purchase.

MARGIN CALL: A demand by the lender that a loan be reduced because the value of the assets pledged has been reduced.

MARGIN MAINTENANCE: The margin required by a lender. If that margin is not maintained, the assets will be sold.

MARGIN SALE: Assets sold because a margin call was not met.

MARKET: A like group of transactions.

MARKETABLE: The salability of an asset.

MATURITY: The date when a contract comes due.

MONETARY INFLATION: An increase in the supply of money.

MONEY: A medium of exchange that is readily accepted.

MONEY MARKET FUND: A short-term mutual fund that invests only in interest-bearing securities.

MONEY SUPPLY: The total of a our country's currency. Controlled entirely by the Federal Reserve.

MORATORIUM: A legal delay on the payment of an obligation.

MUTUAL FUND: A company that invests its stockholders' money in other investments. The important aspect of a mutual fund is that its shares have to be redeemed immediately upon request and at net value.

NEGOTIABLE INSTRUMENT: An asset, represented by certificate, that can be readily sold.

PAR: The stated value.

PAR VALUE: The face value of a currency or security.

PORTFOLIO: The total investments of an individual or corporation.

PREMIUM: The amount that an asset is sold for above its value or sale price.

PRIME RATE: The loan rate banks charge their best commercial customers. This is the banker's definition.

PURCHASING POWER: The value of money expressed by the value of the goods the money can purchase.

PUT OPTION: The right to sell an asset at a predetermined price any time before a certain agreed upon date.

REDEMPTION: The repurchasing of a security by the issuer.

RESERVE: Money put aside for the possibility of paying future losses. In some cases, like a bank's Loan Loss Reserve, a reserve is required by law or statute.

RESISTANCE LEVEL: A price level at which selling is anticipated.

ROUND LOT: The minimum volume of trading that does not incur special trading fees. Often refers to 100 shares of stock.

SAFEKEEPING ACCOUNT: An account where one stores the assets of another.

SECURED LOAN: A loan that involves pledged assets.

SECURITY: In an investment sense, a certificate representing money entrusted to another.

SHORT SALE: The selling of a borrowed security.

SPECULATION: An investment that involves a high probability of loss.

SPOT PRICE: The price for an immediate sale of an asset.

SPREAD: The difference between the asked and the bid price.

STOP-LOSS ORDER: The order to sell an asset if it drops to a certain price level.

STOP ORDER TO BUY: The order to buy an asset if it reaches a certain price level.

STRIKING PRICE: The price at which a warrant holder may buy an asset.

TAX: Money taken from its owner by some form of government.

TAX HAVEN: A country that offers tax advantages to foreigners.

TIME DEPOSIT: A deposit at your bank that cannot be withdrawn until a certain date. Early withdrawal is assessed a penalty in money or interest.

TRADE BALANCE: A nation's exports minus imports. Balance of trade payments occur when imports exceed exports. Over the long term this can be dangerous to a country's economy.

TRADING: The buying and selling of assets.

UNEARNED INCOME: Nonsalary income. For example: interest, royalties, and dividends.

UPSIDE POTENTIAL: The reasonable expectation of the increasing value of an asset.

WARRANT: An option to purchase an asset at a fixed price on a predetermined date.

WEALTH: Usable resources.

Although this glossary is not extensive, it should assist your understanding of the market. However, don't see these definitions as the parameters of the Rational Investing concept. By definition, a glossary explains things not readily understood. In this case that means, for the most part, stock market terms and all associated investment terminology. You, on the other hand, should realize that your market may be investment grade coins or stamps, real estate, or whatever. This note is added so no one gives investment significance to my glossary. It gives no indication of preference. It only explains terms you might find confusing.

Assistance Directory

The relationship between an investor and his or her broker is one of trust. The fiduciary nature of the broker's responsibility means he or she must be held to the highest standard of professional conduct. Yet, as history continually proves, too many brokers use questionable practices. This happens at even the largest and most respected brokerage firms.

Fortunately, there are agencies to help a victimized investor. Whether your complaint is account churning, an unsuitable investment, or not processing your trades on time or correctly, if you feel abused you have no recourse but to try to recover what monies you lost due to the broker's inappropriate actions. Once you have decided to pursue the matter, you have to know where to turn. The following list will help:

1. Try to resolve matters with the broker directly. If he or she isn't able or willing to arrange an outcome that meets your satisfaction, contact an officer of the house.

State your complaint in writing. Outline the action you want the house to take to make things right. Make sure to keep copies of all correspondence.

The vast majority of problems are resolved at this level. Legitimate brokers and their house don't want trouble and possible bad publicity, so you do have leverage with your complaint. They don't need the irritation. According to my research, 85 percent of all complaints are resolved directly between the client and the house.

It is sad that more investors don't pursue matters when they believe they have been wronged. Too many, apparently not realizing they have recourse available, don't bother. Others are too intimidated to seek restitution.

2. Your next line of defense is your state securities officer. Most governmental actions against brokers are processed by this agency. To contact the office in your state, write or call The North American Securities Administration Association, 555 New Jersey Ave., NW, Suite 750, Washington, DC 20001, (202) 737-0900. They will give you the number to call in your state.

3. On a federal level, The Securities and Exchange Commission (SEC) and the Commodity Futures Trading Commission (CFTC) are available depending on the nature of the difficulty. Write or call the SEC, Consumer Affairs, 450 15th St. NW, Washington, DC 20549 (202) 272-7440, or CFTC, Office of Public Information, 2033 K St., NW, Washington, DC 20581, (202) 254-8630.

4. Complaints regarding the sale of futures should be addressed to the National Futures Association, Consumer Affairs, 200 W. Madison St., Suite 1600, Chicago, IL 60606, (800) 621-3570.

5. Complaints regarding brokerage houses on specific exchanges should be addressed to that exchange's discipline committee. Write or call the New York Stock Exchange, 11 Wall St., New York, NY 10005, (212) 656–3000.

American Stock Exchange, 86 Trinity Place, New York, NY 10006, (212) 306–1000. Boston Stock Exchange, 1 Boston Pl., Boston, MA 02108, (617) 723–9500. Cincinnati Stock Exchange, 205 Dixie Terminal, Cincinnati, OH 45202 (513) 621–1410. Midwest Stock Exchange, 440 S. LaSalle St., Chicago, IL 60605, (312) 663–2222. Pacific Stock Exchange, 301 Pine St., San Francisco, CA 94104, (415) 393–4000. Philadelphia Stock Exchange, 1900 Market St., Philadelphia, PA 10103, (215) 496–5000.

6. Complaints against brokers should be addressed to the self-policing trade agency, National Association of Securities Dealers (NASD), Surveillance Dept., 1735 K St., NW, Washington, DC 20006, (202) 728–8000.

7. If you have a problem with your broker and a commodity transaction, you should direct your complaint to the agency representing that specific exchange where the trade(s) took place. Chicago Options Exchange, LaSalle at Van Buren, Chicago, IL 60605, (312) 786–5600. Chicago Board of Trade, 141 W. Jackson Blvd., Chicago, IL 60604, (312) 435–3500. Chicago Mercantile Exchange, 30 S. Wacker Drive, Chicago, IL 60606, (312) 930–8200. New York Futures Exchange, 20 Broad St., New York, NY 10004, (212) 623–4949. New York Cotton Exchange, 4 World Trade Center, New York, NY 10048, (212) 938–2650. New York Mercantile Exchange, 4 World Trade Center, New York, NY 10048, (212) 938–2222. Commodity Exchange, Inc., 4 World Trade Center, New York, NY 10048, (212) 938–2900. Kansas City Board of Trade,

4800 W. Main St., Suite 303, Kansas City, MO 64112,
(816) 753-7500.

As an investor, you cannot afford to let your broker, or
anyone else for that matter, cost you money if his or her
actions were unprofessional or illegal. If you're not sure,
and the matter is only questionable, pursue it anyway.
Let the appropriate agency determine the legalities involved.

Remember, you have nonarbitration remedies at your
disposal. The previous addresses should help direct your
efforts.

In some cases it may be necessary or wise to write a
number of the agencies available regarding the same
issue. Although you don't want a shotgun approach, it is
more productive to involve as many responsible parties
as possible. This increases your leverage with the offend-
ing broker or house.

Of course, after exhausting all your immediately available options, you must remember your right to arbitration. It, as explained earlier, may be your only tangible
recourse. However, as the previous listing indicates, it's
not your only one. You should explore every alternative
prior to becoming involved in the industry-controlled arbitration process.

No matter what your course of action, I hope you resolve
to correct any investment matter where you believe you
have been financially injured. Doing nothing costs you
money and helps perpetuate unprofessional broker conduct. My consulting experience clearly indicates that *an
aggressive investor can right almost any wrong* in a broker
dispute.

A Case Study

There could be no tougher test for the ability of Rational Investing to make money than the Crash of '87.

On that day most investors lost not only their previously earned profits, but goodly portions of their capital as well. Immediately prior to that historic event, the market had experienced a record-breaking bull run. From January 1 to Black Monday the stock market had increased almost 40 percent in value, so it was not surprising that many made more money in the market than ever before. Unfortunately, that caused them to believe that they knew what they were doing. They didn't. They simply were at the right place at the right time. Their success wasn't a reflection of their ability, but rather a matter of happenstance. Look at Figure A-1.

You can see why those in the market in the months prior to October 1987 did quite well. The totals at the beginning of the month clearly illustrate that the market was experiencing a euphoria of overvaluation, and every-

FIGURE A-1
Dow-Jones Averages for 1987

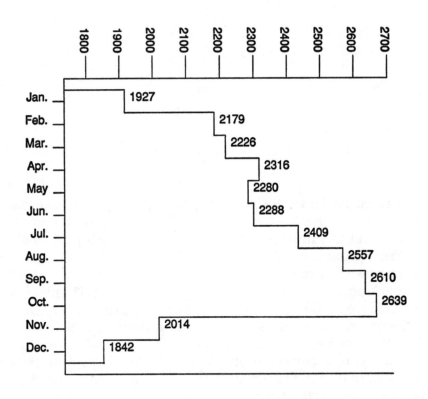

one that played the game profited. But is that the essence
of investing? Hardly. You cannot forget that INVESTING

IS A LIFETIME CONSIDERATION. Short-term profits are nice, but winning consistently is how your efforts are ultimately judged. Proof of that criterion was felt on October 19, 1987. The market took back most, if not all, it had given. For the majority of individual investors, it took back more than it gave. The market proved once again that it is a house game by collapsing for no legitimate reason. It faltered because it was overvalued, and it was overvalued because it has little basis in economic reality. Companies saw their stock value as much as halved in a matter of hours when in actuality nothing had changed back at the office. The point being, the market, which is supposed to be a yardstick of America's corporate health, was manipulated by the brokerage houses, traders, brokers, and other insiders. That's how the overvaluation occurred. It was manufactured. And that's why the market collapsed. I mention this again because of the importance of the message.

The collapse is a perfect example of why I repeatedly have made an effort to redefine the word market. Investments come in many shapes and forms. Rare coins, real estate, personal lending, precious metals, small business, and collectible investments didn't collapse in October of '87—the stock market did. Remember that when you decide where to invest your money.

This case study uses the stock market because the year of the Crash is an excellent, extremely difficult test for Rational Investing. If it made money while the market experienced record reversals, perhaps you'll see the wisdom of its application. To accomplish this test I had to assign a dollar value to a mythical mutual fund. It's subsequent value is determined by the value of the market in general. Look at Figure A-2.

You'll notice the chart corresponds with Figure A-1. I began with a unit value of five dollars, which is nothing more than a representational, yet arbitrary choice. The

---

FIGURE A-2
Dow-Jones Averages for 1987
Converted to a Mutual Fund
($5.00 Original Price)

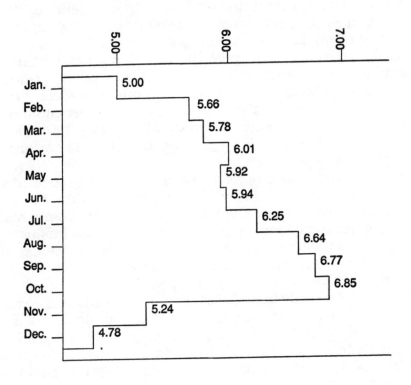

future value of the fund's units is then determined by the actual Dow-Jones valuation in the corresponding month. If the market went up 10 percent that month I raised the unit valuation 10 percent. Figure A-2 is a direct reflection of the market between the months of January through December 1987.

There is an interesting and important aspect of this time period. It is perhaps the worst imaginable for Rational Investing. Why? As I've said throughout this book, the plan works because it recognizes the cycles of markets. During this time span, there was no cycle. The market went virtually straight up; then it went straight down. Fortunately, this happens very rarely. Then too, this short time span further hurts the plan's results. Rational Investing works best over an extended time, as I have explained. Regardless, these are two events that work against the program. The value of any investment plan can best be determined in a worst case scenario, and the Crash makes the point regarding Rational Investing's value.

The test is as follows: I have taken ten thousand dollars and invested in the market. Table A-1 reflects how that investment fared using the standard investment technique of buying stock, sitting back, and hoping for the best. Table A-2 reflects how the investment fared using Rational Investing. In each example I invested another two hundred dollars each month. In Table A-1 the two hundred dollars was used to buy more stock. In Table A-2 it's used to buy one hundred dollars worth of units and add one hundred dollars to our cash valuation.

The bottom line for the traditional investment approach was a yearly return (loss) of (7.71 percent) That was arrived at by the combination of the best and worst the market could offer; i.e., the record-breaking run up and the Crash. But did the market actually lose 7.71 percent during this time? In a generic sense, yes. In a personal

Table A-1
Traditional Market Investment Technique
Dow Jones Averages for 1987

1987	Market Purchases	Increase (Decrease) Over Rest of Year	Dollar Value at Year End
January	10,200	(4.4)	9,751.20
February	200	(15.5)	169.00
March	200	(17.3)	165.40
April	200	(20.5	159.00
May	200	(19.2)	161.60
June	200	(19.4)	161.20
July	200	(23.5)	153.00
August	200	(27.9)	144.20
September	200	(29.4)	141.20
October	200	(30.2)	139.60
November	200	(8.5)	183.00
December	200	–	200.00
TOTAL	$12,400		$11,528.40

1. Total Invested $12,400.00
2. Total Return   11,528.40
3. Profit (Loss)   (871.60)
4. Average Investment   11,300.00
5. Yearly Yield (Loss)   (7.71)

sense, no. The fact is, many were completely wiped out during the Crash. The 7.71 percent loss is an average of the market as opposed to a reflection of individual investment performance. Many investors would gladly trade

TABLE A-2
The Rational Investor Example for 1987

Unit Price ($)	Portfolio Value ($)	Cash ($)	Units Bought (Sold)	Units Owned	Management Application	Bought (Sold) $ Amount	Interest ($)	Total Investment Value ($)
5.00	5,100	100 5,142	20.0 1,000.0	1,020.0	—	5,100	42	10,242
5.66	5,705	100 5,453	17.7 (29.7)	1,008.0	.033	(168)	43	11,158
5.78	5,704	100 5,820	17.3 (38.4)	986.9	.039	(222)	45	11,524
6.01	5,649	100 6,351	16.6 (63.6)	939.9	.067	(382)	49	12,000
5.92	5,956	100 6,212	16.9 49.3	1,006.1	.046	292	53	12,168
5.94	5,796	100 6,644	16.8 (47.1)	975.8	.047	(280)	52	12,440
6.25	5,718	100 7,280	16.0 (77.0)	914.8	.083	(481)	55	12,998
6.64	5,236	100 8,379	15.1 (141.3)	788.6	.0164	(938)	61	13,615
6.77	4,512	100 9,476	14.8 (136.9)	666.5	.177	(927)	70	13,988

Table Continues

TABLE A-2
(Continued)

Unit Price ($)	Portfolio Value ($)	Cash ($)	Units Bought (Sold)	Units Owned	Management Application	Bought (Sold) $ Amount	Interest	Total Investment Value ($)
		100	14.6					
6.85	3,831	10,490	(121.9)	559.2	.185	(835)	79	14,321
		100	19.1					
5.24	3,136	10,577	20.2	598.5	.010	106	87	13,707
		100	20.9					
4.78	3,056	10,657	19.9	639.3	.009	95	88	13,713

1. $10,000 original investment
2. $100 deposited to CASH each month. $100 worth of UNITS bought each month—top number in UNITS BOUGHT (SOLD)
3. Total invested—$12,400. Average investment—$11,300.
4. Return—$1,313. Yield—11.6%

their record during this time for a 7.71 percent loss. It would have saved them perhaps tens of thousands of dollars.

Rational Investing, during the same time with the same investment, made a yearly return of 11.6 percent. It turned the market, a loser during this time, into a winner. Between the two approaches you have an 19.31 point swing! And that remarkable differential was accomplished by this very simple and effective account management technique.

Clearly you should not be satisfied with a return of 11.6 percent, but that's not the point of this illustration. The point is: the plan beat the market, as it, over the long term, almost always does. However, to put things in perspective, an 11.6 percent return during one of the worst stock market debacles in history isn't to be ignored. Rational Investing made a respectable return at a time when most investors were in the process of experiencing a substantial, if not total, loss.

The plan is reflective of the market in which it is employed. This model has been proof of that point. If your investment vehicle or market is down, the plan will return less than it would have had the market been status quo or up. But, and this is crux of the matter, regardless of the return, Rational Investing does exactly what it says it will— it maximizes profits.

Contacting the Author

To reach me with any comments, questions, or consulting needs, write Reliance Enterprises, Inc., P.O. Box 413, Marengo, IL 60152.

Finally, I would like to respectfully recommend that you consider a subscription to my newsletter. *Money Insider* is dedicated to giving you the confidential information your stockbroker, banker, lawyer, and others don't want you to have. Additionally, I know you'll be pleased with the uniqueness of our format, the value of our market counsel, and the immediate benefit of each article.

If you would like to review a free issue, send a business size SASE and three dollars for handling to Reliance at the above address. To subscribe, send forty-nine dollars for twelve monthly issues to Money Insider, P.O. Box 12269, Boulder, CO 80303–0070.

Index